DATE DUE			

HOW TO BORROW MONEY

HOW TO BORROW MONEY

Oliver G. Wood, Jr.
Professor of Banking and Finance
University of South Carolina

and

William C. Barksdale, Jr.
Senior Vice President and
Administrator of Commercial Loans
The South Carolina National Bank

VNR VAN NOSTRAND REINHOLD COMPANY
NEW YORK   CINCINNATI   ATLANTA   DALLAS   SAN FRANCISCO
LONDON   TORONTO   MELBOURNE

Van Nostrand Reinhold Company Regional Offices:
New York   Cincinnati   Atlanta   Dallas   San Francisco

Van Nostrand Reinhold Company International Office:
London   Toronto   Melbourne

Library of Congress Catalog Card Number: 80-25468
ISBN: 0-442-25204-8

Manufactured in the United States of America

Published by Van Nostrand Reinhold Company
135 West 50th Street, New York, N.Y. 10020

Published simultaneously in Canada by Van Nostrand Reinhold Ltd.

15   14   13   12   11   10   9   8   7   6   5   4   3   2   1

Library of Congress Cataloging in Publication Data
Wood, Oliver G.   1937-
   How to borrow money.

   Includes index.
   1. Credit—Handbooks, manuals, etc.   I. Barksdale,
William C., joint author.   II. Title.
HG3751.W66   658.1'5224   80-25468
ISBN 0-442-25204-8

For

Milledge B. Seigler, Ph.D.
Distinguished Professor Emeritus of English
University of South Carolina

With Our Deepest Respect and Gratitude

PREFACE

This book is designed to help any person or business that needs to borrow money now or sometime in the future.

Knowing how to borrow money is essential to financial survival. The person with the courage to enter business today has to be able to cope with costs rising at a double-digit pace, mountains of government regulations and red tape, and low productivity in the work force. In spite of all this, the business manager has to battle competition, make a profit, and somehow always have enough money in the bank to meet the payroll and other required payments. At one time or another, every business has to borrow to meet these financial obligations. This book can help you solve your money problems.

The authors of this book have 20 years combined experience analyzing and approving loan requests at banks. We have seen first-hand that the person who knows how to borrow usually gets the money he or she needs. Knowing how to borrow money means knowing *why and when* to borrow, *how much* to borrow, and *how to pay* it back. Too many times we have seen loan requests fail because the borrower did not understand the borrowing process. Out of this experience came the idea to write a book that will help make people successful borrowers and take the mystery and fear out of borrowing.

We gratefully acknowledge the assistance of those who worked with us on this book. Gloria Hicks and Frances Donnelly typed the manuscript accurately and cheerfully. Attorneys Jean Bissell and Steve Lynch clarified a number of technical points. Patricia Wood provided many creative ideas and invaluable help in getting the book in final form.

OLIVER G. WOOD, JR.
WILLIAM C. BARKSDALE, JR.

CONTENTS

HOW TO BORROW MONEY

1
How This Book Can Help You

By purchasing this book, you have taken a giant step toward learning how to obtain money to expand an existing business or to start a new business. Knowledge is power! Money is power! The number one goal of this book is to provide you with the knowledge to obtain money—the source of financial power.

Every business in America borrows money. General Motors, the automotive giant, has outstanding debts of over $13 billion. Exxon, the world's most profitable company, owes over $21 billion. It is not bad business to borrow money. In fact, borrowing is good business, providing you know: (1) how much money to borrow and on what terms, (2) how to use borrowed money profitably and wisely, and (3) how to exercise the financial discipline necessary to ensure timely repayment.

THE FOUR BUSINESS FUNCTIONS

Every business performs four functions:

1. *Production*— the manufacturing of goods and/or the providing of services.
2. *Marketing*—the selling of goods and services.
3. *Personnel*—the management of the "people resources" in the business.
4. *Finance*—the acquisition and utilization of monetary resources.

You probably started your business because you felt that there was a need for a particular product or service and because you had confidence that you could produce and market that which would fill this need. In other words, you believed that you had a special ability in the first two functions—production and marketing.

Most business managers also believe that they can handle the personnel function without any special training. This may be false confidence because in today's "what's in it for me" society getting people to produce and work together is not an easy task. Moreover, the personnel function has become increasingly complicated by a maze of federal and state regulations. A good people manager in today's environment must have a blend of experience from the "school of hard knocks" and a good knowledge of governmental regulations applicable to personnel.

Of the four basic business functions, the finance function is the one about which most businessmen are least knowledgeable. Finance is the "tag-along" function, but if you fumble finance, you can be out of business in no time flat. In most cases, people do not start businesses because they know how to borrow and utilize money effectively. As stated earlier they usually start a business because they are talented in production or marketing. Typically, this experience was acquired in another company's production or marketing division. Any experience gained in finance was "on the side" and probably quite superficial and incomplete.

It is with a special part of the fourth function—the art and science of borrowing money—that we hope this book will help you. How you *utilize* the money you borrow will depend largely on your ability to purchase raw material and inventory, schedule production, hire people, sell the product or provide the service, and collect receivables. This book is not about those tasks (but we manage to slip in some words of advice here and there). You are the expert in those areas. However, this book can teach you just about everything you need to know about borrowing money.

Here is a list of 7 important aspects about borrowing money that are covered in this book. You will learn:

1. How to analyze your needs for money (Chapters 2 and 3)

First, this involves a determination of whether you need money for short-term purposes or long-term purposes. Short-term loans should be for short-term purposes such as meeting current expenses, purchasing inventory, or carrying accounts receivable. Long-term loans should be for long-term purposes such as the expansion of fixed assets, expansion of current assets to support higher sales and profit levels, or perhaps refinancing of assets to enable a business to recover from a business recession or a natural disaster.

2. Where to apply for loans (Chapter 4)

There are an assortment of lenders. Some, such as savings and loan associations, specialize in real estate loans. Others, such as commercial banks, make all kinds of loans. There are major differences among lenders with respect to the terms of credit, that is, interest rates, maturity, and collateral. Thus, *where* you borrow does make a difference. In Chapter 4, we will examine in detail the nature and characteristics of the primary sources of money such as commercial banks, commercial finance companies, vendors, and leasing companies.

3. How to apply for loans (Chapter 5)

Many people are frightened stiff by the prospect of sitting down face-to-face with a loan officer and asking for a loan. However, underneath this fear is ignorance. There is nothing to fear if you know: (1) how to contact the appropriate lender and discuss your cash needs, (2) what information and material to provide the lender, and (3) what questions to anticipate so you will have ready answers. Chapter 5 provides you with a step-by-step approach to how to apply for the money you need.

4. What the lender will do with your application (Chapter 6)

Most people do not like the thought of a lender investigating how much they earn or their paying record. However, when an institution lends money, it becomes a partner with the borrower in all of his or her endeavors and shares in both good and bad fortunes. Therefore, it is only natural to expect that a lender will look into a borrower's ability and willingness to repay the money. In Chapter 6, you will learn the various steps taken by the lender to process your loan application. This will enable you to do two things: (1) to understand better the borrowing/lending process and (2) allow you to provide better and more timely information that will improve your chances of having your loan request approved.

5. *What happens at the loan closing* (Chapter 7)

People who attended the loan closing for the purchase of their home usually come out of it saying that it was one of their most unforgettable experiences and that they do not want to go through it again. They could not believe the number of documents that they were confronted with and *had to sign* to get the money. In Chapter 7 we will take you step-by-step through a loan closing and explain the general nature of every document that is involved.

6. *What happens after you get the money* (Chapter 8)

After a business borrower obtains the loan proceeds, he has three major responsibilities: (1) comply with the loan agreement, (2) monitor closely his own performance and utilization of the borrowed money, and (3) keep the lender informed of his performance through timely financial statements and oral reports. Contrary to what you might believe, if things did start going badly in your business, it would be best to inform the lender immediately. Lenders usually are quite flexible and willing to restructure loan terms or delay or reduce payments in order to enable you to work out of your difficulties. An experienced business loan officer can be invaluable to you in counseling you on how to solve your problems because he deals every day with businesses that cannot pay on time. In Chapter 8 you will learn how to monitor your own performance and what steps you should take to keep your lender informed and happy.

7. How to survive during tough times (Chapter 9)

We do not have to tell you that times can be tough for business. Double-digit inflation, double-digit interest rates, intermittent recession, declining productivity, the energy crunch, and international tension plague business. All of these phenomena have one thing in common for the average business—they reduce profit margins and the ability of firms to meet their loan obligations on time. In Chapter 9 we will analyze the financial difficulties that you can incur during these tough times and make a list of action steps that you can take to improve your chances of financial survival.

2

Short-Term Money For Short-Term Purposes

A business' cash needs may be classified as short-term or long-term. Short-term cash needs are those that occur within a one-year time horizon. Long-term cash needs are those that extend beyond one year. In this chapter we will: (1) examine the nature and importance of cash, (2) learn how to use a cash budget to determine cash needs, (3) demonstrate with a simple business example the interrelationship among cash flows, the income statement, and the statement of condition, and (4) describe the precautionary and speculative motives for holding money.

CASH AND CASH NEEDS

Nature of Money

You probably are wondering why we are going to tell you what cash is and why it is important. But would you believe that so many important developments have taken place in finance in recent years that the Federal Reserve is not really sure what money is? With respect to the importance of cash, in a world with rapid inflation, many people would tell you that cash is an undesirable asset. We think differently; cash is very important, probably more so than when times were less financially turbulent.

What is cash or money? There are many definitions, but try this one: *Money is anything commonly used and generally accepted in exchange for goods and services and for the payment of debts.* The word "anything" is used to avoid restriction. As we shall see, several items serve as money in our economy. The term "commonly used" indicates that we wish to exclude things that are occasionally used, such as cigarettes.

A number of items serve as money in the United States. The following are the major types of money.

Major Types of Money

1. Federal Reserve notes (currency)
2. coins
3. demand deposits at commercial banks

Federal Reserve notes are issued by Federal Reserve Banks to commercial banks which issue them to people and businesses that need currency to effect small day-to-day transactions. *Coins* are issued by the Treasury to the Federal Reserve Banks which issue them to commercial banks which issue them to people and businesses that need them for daily transactions. Currency and coin constitute 38 percent of the money supply.

Demand deposits simply are credits on the books of commercial banks. We use *checks* as orders to banks to transfer these bookkeeping credits to the payee designated on the check. Most people do not understand the origin of demand deposits. A bank creates these deposits when it makes a loan. Suppose that Bill's TV Repair has the opportunity to buy $10,000 of electronic parts from a bankrupt shop. Bill goes down to the bank and signs a six-month note. At that time, Bill hands the loan officer a deposit slip from his checkbook. The loan officer writes in "$10,000 loan proceeds" and hands the slip to a teller who puts it in with the daily work for the bookkeeping department. A keypunch operator punches out a card with a +$10,000 credit in the Bill's TV Repair demand deposit account. With this entry, demand deposits have been created.

Republic National Bank		Bill's TV Repair	
Assets	*Liabilities*	*Assets*	*Liabilities*
Loan + $10,000	Demand deposit (Bill's TV Repair) + $10,000)	Demand deposit at RNB + $10,000	Loan from RNB + $10,000

Notice on the balance sheets above that the bank now has a new asset (the loan) and a new liability (demand deposits payable to Bill's TV Repair). Bill's TV Repair has a new asset (the demand deposit) and a new liability (the loan).

Many people think that when a bank makes a loan, it lends "other people's deposits." This is a big misconception. The bank simply creates the money. This money, in the form of bookkeeping credits, is transferred among people and businesses by means of checks. These bank bookkeeping credits comprise 72 percent of our money. When a borrower repays a loan, he simply writes a check payable to the bank for the amount of the loan plus interest. The bank then decreases demand deposits and marks the loan paid. Thus, in our banking system demand deposits increase when loans are made and decrease when loans are paid.

There are several other types of financial claims that are very similar to demand deposits. These claims are known as *near money* because they can be converted quite easily into demand deposits. Moreover, in recent years, techniques have been developed to allow people to use near monies to pay for goods and services and pay debts. Here is a list of important near monies.

Major Types of Near Money

Type	*Institutions Issuing*
1. Time and savings deposits, money market certificates	Commercial banks Savings and loan associations Mutual savings banks Credit unions
2. Money-market mutual fund shares	Money market mutual funds

Time and savings deposits at banks, savings and loan associations, and credit unions are the primary form of near money. Unlike demand deposits, these claims earn interest. Time deposits in the form of *certificates of deposit* (CDs) have fixed maturities which make them "not-so-near money." However, *passbook savings deposits* may be transferred quite easily into bank demand deposits. At a bank, all you have to do is fill out a withdrawal slip for the savings deposit and a deposit slip to transfer the deposits into your demand deposit account. Some banks have a telephone transfer arrangement that permits a customer to call in and make transfers between savings and demand deposit accounts. At savings and loan associations, mutual savings banks and credit unions, savers making withdrawals receive a bank check which can be deposited in a bank demand deposit. Some of these nonbank savings institutions have telephone transfer systems and a number of credit unions permit savers to write *share drafts* (similar to checks) on their accounts. On January 1, 1981, banks and nonbank savings institutions across the country began offering NOW accounts which permit savers to earn interest on their deposits and use a check-like instrument called a *negotiable order of withdrawal* (NOW) to make transfers of funds.

The newest near money is *money market mutual fund shares*. With interest rates at historical highs, people and businesses recognized that holding noninterest-bearing currency and demand deposits had a high opportunity cost in terms of foregone interest. A number of mutual funds have been established that sell shares to the public and take the money and invest it in short-term high-yielding million dollar certificates of deposit. These funds pay daily interest and permit shareholders to transfer balances to others by means of *drafts*. These are check-like instruments that are orders to pay money, in this case when the draft reaches the mutual fund's bank.

As you can see, several of the above near monies are really close to meeting our definition of money. Today, people and businesses are using telephone transfer arrangements, share drafts, NOWs,

and drafts on money market mutual funds to pay for goods and
services and pay debts. You must be aware of these financial inno-
vations as you manage your business' cash budget.

Importance of Money

We are sure that you have a smile on your face after reading the
above heading and are murmuring to yourself, "You bet it is."
Yes, money is a great asset. Some people would say that it is the
"ultimate asset."

Money has a number of qualities that make it desirable. First,
and perhaps most importantly, money is the only asset generally
accepted in payment for goods and services and for debts. Land,
stocks, bonds, and stamp collections are not generally accepted.
Thus, people and businesses have a demand for money to buy
items needed every day. This demand is sometimes called the
transactions demand for money. The primary basis for this demand for money stems from the lack of synchronization between
the inflows and outflows of money. If, every time you needed to
pay a bill, you always had a cash sale or collected a receivable
equal to the amount you owed, then there would be no transactions demand for money. Since both money inflows and outflows
are not perfectly predictable, it is necessary to plan and budget for
money needs in order to avoid financial embarrassment.

Finally, money is attractive as a *form of wealth*. If people expect the value of stocks, bonds, land, or other popular forms of
wealth to decline, then money offers an attractive alternative. Besides having a fixed face value, money offers flexibility through
its liquidity, that quality which enables an asset holder to shift
quickly and without loss to another form of wealth.

CASH BUDGETING

For a Person

The only reason a person needs to borrow is that he or she is short
of money. People have two basic short-run purposes for needing

money: to pay what they owe and to buy what they need. There are many factors that can cause a person to be cash short; however, they all stem from an imbalance between the inflows and outflows of cash. In order to survive economically, a person, no matter how wealthy or poor, must match inflows and outflows of cash so that inflows of cash consistently exceed outflows. The above concepts also apply to a business. Let's continue our analogy by looking at the management of a personal checking account.

An individual usually has a predictable inflow from wages. In addition, he or she typically incurs an equally predictable stream of bills that must be paid. As long as wages coming in exceed checks being written, the checking account always has money in it. Of course, it sometimes has more than at other times, but nonetheless, it has a positive balance.

At times, a person may need to meet a cash demand greater than the balance in his or her checking account. Examples of such needs include buying a car, replacing a major appliance, meeting unexpected and uninsured medical or dental bills, buying a seasonal wardrobe, or paying educational expenses.

What does the individual do when such expenses arise and extra cash is needed? Ask for a raise? Surely not, but some might try. Normally, only one of two courses of action are available: dip into savings or borrow the needed money. If savings are available when a major expense is incurred, so much the better. But what if savings are not available? The only course left is either postpone the cash outflow or borrow funds from some available source to meet it.

If an individual must borrow, he or she must demonstrate both a willingness and an ability to repay the loan. The willingness may be there, but if the need is considerable, it may be difficult to convince the lender that the loan should be granted.

It is the borrower's task to prove to the lender that the loan can be repaid. The lender will require a financial statement, credit references, and possibly collateral to serve as a secondary source of repayment if the borrower cannot meet his or her payments. At the same time, the borrower may be revising the family budget, thinking about moonlighting, or sending his or her spouse out to find work.

This example could be followed *ad nauseum* with a description of every conceivable need for cash, but it will not be. It has been used only to demonstrate a few very important points:

1. You cannot spend more than you make.
2. If you do, you must dip into savings or sell something you own to get cash.
3. If you cannot get the needed cash from savings or converting something you own into cash, you borrow the needed cash if you can demonstrate your ability and willingness to repay the loan and, if necessary, make the lender secure with collateral.

With respect to those personal, unplanned cash outlays that necessitate borrowing, how does an ordinary individual keep ordinary cash inflows and outflows in balance? The answer is with a time-honored technique known as *personal* or *family budgeting*. First, this process involves making monthly estimates of cash inflows from wages or salary, interest, dividends, or rent. Second, it involves monthly outlays for rent or the mortgage payment, food, clothing, gas, utilities, and so on. Third, you subtract the outflows from the inflows in order to determine how much is available for saving. If in some months the anticipated outlays exceed the inflows, then we are back to the solution suggested earlier—dip into savings or borrow.

For a Business

The same description of cash budgeting for a person or a family applies to any business, whether it is Exxon or Bill's TV Repair. Each business needs cash "to pay what it owes" or "buy what it needs." When businesses are unable to pay what they owe or buy what they need, they must borrow. Just as a person must prepare a budget of "cash in" and "cash out," so must a business. Business cash budgets range from simple worksheets to complicated computer models. The degree of complexity also depends on the number of cash inflow and cash inflow producing departments.

Business cash budgeting involves planning and forecasting all monthly cash inflows and outflows over a short-term period such as a year. A cash budget is vital because it reveals both the magnitude and the timing of needed borrowing. The first step in the preparation of a business cash budget is to plan and forecast monthly cash flows. Here are examples of major cash inflows and outflows.

A. *Cash Inflows*
1. Cash sales
2. Collection of accounts receivable
3. Income tax refunds
4. Proceeds from selling used equipment
5. Proceeds from the sale of any other asset
6. Recovery of bad debts that have been charged off

B. *Cash Outflows*
1. Purchase inventory
2. Payment of current operating expenses
3. Payment of fixed expenses
4. Make installment payments on loans
5. Payment of taxes
6. Payment of dividends

Table 2-1 contains a sample consolidated cash budget for three months.

Steps in Business Cash Budgeting

1. Prepare monthly sales forecast. Forecasting future inflows and outflows must begin with a monthly sales forecast. Get a piece of graph paper and plot monthly sales over the last two or three years. Then fit a freehand line to these monthly sales figures and extend the line over the next 12 months. This line may be adjusted upward or downward to reflect the impact of expected de-

Table 2-1. Sample Cash Budget.
(in thousands of dollars)

| | Month Ending | | |
	Dec. 31	Jan. 31	Feb. 28
Beginning Cash	20	20	20
Plus:			
Cash Sales	100	60	90
Receivables Collections	18	15	15
Recovery of Bad Debts	2	2	1
Cash Available	140	97	126
Less:			
Purchase of Inventory	70	100	60
Operating Expenses	15	12	14
Fixed Expenses	10	10	10
Cash Needed	95	122	84
Net Cash Available	+ 45	− 25	+ 42
Bank Loan (+)		45	
Loan Payment (−)	(25)		(22)
Ending Cash	20	20	20

velopments such as increased or decreased competition and new products or services or the loss of same. This simple trend extension technique works best for businesses without strong seasonal patterns of sales. If there is a strong seasonal pattern it is just too difficult to sketch in the sales line. An alternative technique is to simply list past monthly sales, forecast the percentage increase in monthly sales, and calculate monthly numerical sales forecasts.

  2. Estimate inflows from receivables. The volume of monthly receivables that a business collects depends upon: (1) the general level of credit sales, (2) the terms of these sales, and (3) the vigor behind collection efforts. Close analysis of most firms' monthly collection of receivables will reveal a percentage relationship between collections and the previous one, two, and three months' credit sales. For example, a business may find that this month's collections equal 90 percent of last month's credit sales, nine percent of credit sales from the month before last, and one percent slow payers and bad debts. Hence, after this relationship is determined, the firm can use this information together with a forecast of credit sales to estimate this element of the monthly cash inflow.

3. Estimate other cash inflows. Other cash inflows occur at odd times during the year. Generally you know from previous years when to expect your tax refund, if any. However, the receipt of money from the sale of used equipment and other assets usually can be planned to occur within a short time frame, so these inflows may be entered on the cash budget with some degree of certainty. Finally, recoveries of bad debts have a predictable and an unpredictable element in them. Usually some small inflows occur every month and are a function of earlier sales levels. Analyze the relationship between credit sales and recoveries and make an estimate of the level of expected recoveries. For unpredictable recoveries, do not attempt to estimate them. Treat them as a windfall and do not celebrate until the check clears!

4. Estimate sales-related monthly outflows. Turning to the outflows side of a cash budget, inventory purchases and direct operating expenses such as wages and salaries are directly related to expected sales. Take your last income statement and calculate what percentage of sales each direct expense item is. To forecast each expense item, multiply this percentage by monthly forecasted sales and enter the result in the cash budget.

5. Estimate other cash outflows. Most other cash outflows are recurring and, therefore, predictable. These include fixed expenses such as rent and utilities. These may be entered directly in the cash budget. Other outflows such as taxes and dividends depend on the level of profits, but they still should be estimated and entered in the cash budget.

6. Set the minimum cash balance. The next step is to set the minimum amount of cash to keep in your demand deposit account. Under many loan agreements, borrowers are required to keep *compensating balances.* These are deposits equal to some percentage of the outstanding loan. This deposit-to-loan percentage may be expressed as a minimum or an average balance to be maintained. A typical minimum percentage is 15 percent. Thus, if you have a bank loan or line of credit of $100,000, then you might in the typical case have to keep $15,000 on deposit at the bank. Thus, such compensating balance requirements form the minimum cash balance target for the cash budget. This target may be above or below the amount that you feel is necessary to operate on comfortably each month. If above, then your target is the compensating balance requirement. If below, then add in a sum and write in the cash target on the bottom line. Do not include in this sum money balances that you would like to hold for contingencies or in lieu of other earning assets or money that will be needed at a future time to buy assets. These money balances should be held in interest-earning form and will be discussed later in the chapter.

7. Calculate monthly loans needed and monthly loan payments. The final step in the preparation of a cash budget is to subtract the outflows from the inflows to determine each month if funds will have to be borrowed or if funds are available to pay loans. If outflows are greater than inflows, then funds must be borrowed to maintain the cash balance target. Of course, if inflows are greater, then debts may be retired. Note in Table 2-1 that in December, the firm expects to have $15,000 available to apply on a loan, but in January, primarily because of a sales decline and larger inventory purchases, it must borrow $45,000 to keep a minimum balance of $20,000.

How to Use a Bank Line of Credit

The typical way a well managed small company borrows money for short-term purposes is under a *bank line of credit.* This is an informal arrangement whereby the bank agrees to lend a business up to some amount, say $100,000, during a period normally a year. Generally, the bank sends you a letter informing you of this privilege, and it is a good idea to acknowledge, in writing, receipt of the line of credit privilege. Wording of such letters varies from bank to bank so make sure you understand all terms and conditions that you must meet to retain this borrowing privilege. Over the course of the year, when the business needs short-term funds, it draws on its line of credit; when it has excess funds, it pays on its line of credit. The loan balance at the bank is sort of like an air box on an accordian; it expands and contracts as funds are borrowed and repaid.

THE NOEL COMPANY EXAMPLE

We have seen how short-term cash needs are determined by use of a cash budget. We now should look at how cash needs unfold over a cash cycle through a year in the life of The NOEL Company, a manufacturer of products for the holiday season.

A *cash cycle* is a process whereby cash is used to purchase raw materials which are manufactured into inventory which, when sold, create accounts receivable which, when collected, become cash again. Cash is tied up throughout the cycle either in raw materials, inventory, or accounts receivable. Beside letting us look at a complete cash cycle, the NOEL example will show the interrelationships among: (1) the cash budget, (2) the balance sheet, and (3) the income statement. Turn to Table 2-2, which contains these three statements for the company, and let's work line by line through this example.

Balance Sheet

Cash
First, look at the line marked cash. Note that except on March 31, NOEL had $20,000 which suggests that the company had a cash management program in effect. On March 31, NOEL had paid all of its bank debt and had an extra $20,000.

Accounts Receivable
Note how receivables declined from $100,000 on December 31 to $5,000 at the end of March and April. This occurred as customers used cash from holiday sales to pay accounts payable to NOEL. From the spring low point, holiday orders began to come in and receivables rose steadily back to the $100,000 level in November and December. Nevertheless, cash remained stable even though collections were high in some months and low in others.

TABLE 2-2. Balance Sheet, Income Statement, and Cash Budget for the NOEL Company (in thousands of dollars)

I. BALANCE SHEET

	DEC. 31	JAN. 31	FEB. 28	MAR. 31	APR. 30	MAY 31	JUN. 30	JUL. 31	AUG. 31	SEP. 30	OCT. 31	NOV. 30	DEC. 31
Assets													
Cash	$ 20	$ 20	$ 20	$ 40	$ 20	$ 20	$ 20	$ 20	$ 20	$ 20	$ 20	$ 20	$ 20
Accounts Receivable	100	80	45	5	5	10	20	30	40	60	80	100	100
Inventory	20	6	3	22	46	70	91	109	121	101	74	43	17
Fixed Assets	50	50	50	50	50	50	50	50	50	50	50	50	50
Total Assets	190	156	118	117	121	150	181	209	231	231	225	213	187
Liabilities													
Bank Debt	60	55	10	0	0	30	60	85	100	105	80	45	0
Accounts Payable	50	10	15	25	30	30	30	30	30	10	10	10	10
Equity	80	91	93	92	91	90	91	94	101	116	135	158	177
Total Liabilities & Equity	190	156	118	117	121	150	181	209	231	231	225	213	187

II. INCOME STATEMENT

	DEC. 31	JAN. 31	FEB. 29	MAR. 31	APR. 30	MAY 31	JUNE 30	JUL. 31	AUG. 31	SEPT. 30	OCT. 31	NOV. 30	DEC. 31
Sales	$ 40	$ 25	$ 10	$ 10	$ 10	$ 15	$ 20	$ 30	$ 50	$ 60	$ 70	$ 60	$ 60
Less:													
COGS [a]	24	18	6	6	6	9	12	18	30	36	42	36	36
Fixed Expenses	5	5	5	5	5	5	5	5	5	5	5	5	5
Profits [b]	11	2	(1)	(1)	(1)	1	3	7	15	19	23	19	19

III. CASH BUDGET

	DEC. 31	JAN. 31	FEB. 29	MAR. 31	APR. 30	MAY 31	JUNE 30	JUL. 31	AUG. 31	SEPT. 30	OCT. 31	NOV. 30	DEC. 31
Beginning Cash	$ 20	$ 20	$ 20	$ 40	$ 20	$ 20	$ 20	$ 20	$ 20	$ 20	$ 20	$ 20	$ 20
Plus:													
Cash Sales and Receivables Collections [c]	60	60	50	10	5	5	10	20	30	40	50	60	60
Cash Available	80	80	70	50	25	25	30	40	50	60	70	80	80
Less:													
Fixed Expenses	5	5	5	5	5	5	5	5	5	5	5	5	5
Payment to Suppliers	50	10	15	25	30	30	30	30	30	10	10	10	10
Cash Disbursements	55	15	20	30	35	35	35	35	35	15	15	15	15
Net Cash Available	25	65	50	20	(10)	(10)	(5)	5	15	45	55	65	65
Bank Loans					30	30	25	15	5				
Loan Payment (−)	(5)	(45)	(10)							(25)	(35)	(45)	(10)
Ending Cash	20	20	40	20	20	20	20	20	20	20	20	20	55

a COGS (Cost of Goods Sold) contains salaries and wages of all production employees.
b For conciseness, we have omitted taxes. In practice, of course, they are a cash outflow.
c For conciseness, no attempt has been made to distinguish "cash sales" from "receivables collection."

19

Inventory

Inventory also follows a seasonal pattern with the low point in February. From this point, NOEL's production line starts rolling and inventory, which begins to pile up in the warehouse, peaks on August 31. Inventory levels decline rapidly in the fall as shipments go out to customers.

Fixed Assets

These assets remain constant throughout the year.

Bank Debt

Bank loans decrease from $60,000 in December to zero in March and April primarily because of the collection of receivables. From the spring "paid out period," bank debt climbs to a seasonal high of $105,000 in September as money must be borrowed to finance the seasonal increase in inventory and receivables.

Accounts Payable

Accounts payable represent short-term, trade credit provided by NOEL's suppliers. Usually when a firm purchases raw material or services, it has 10-30 days to pay. During this period the firm is using trade credit, a source of funds that tends to expand in a seasonal pattern to help fund part of the increase in assets necessary to generate higher sales levels.

Equity

The primary objective of running any business is to maximize shareholders' equity or owners' claims on assets. At NOEL, equity grew very slightly between January and July. However, equity nearly doubled between July and the end of the year.

Income Statement

Sales

NOEL's sales follow a very pronounced seasonal pattern with the peak occurring in October.

Cost of Goods Sold

The cost of direct labor and raw materials is charged to sales; hence, it has an identical seasonal pattern.

Fixed Expenses

Fixed expenses include rent, utilities, officers' salaries, and other outlays that do not vary with sales. For NOEL, the total is $5,000 each month.

Net Profit

NOEL's net profit is negative during the spring off-season. Virtually all of its annual net income is realized during the last four months of the year.

Cash Budget

Now let's see how cash flowed through NOEL over the cash cycle and analyze when it needed to borrow short-term money for short-term purposes.

Beginning Cash

Beginning cash is constant, except in March when excess cash is available.

Cash Sales and Receivables Collection

To save time, NOEL's cash sales and receivables collection are lumped together. However, when you prepare your cash budget, make separate estimates of these cash sources. NOEL's cash receipts begin to pick up in mid-summer and peak during the November to January period.

Cash Available

Cash available includes beginning cash plus cash sales and receivables collection.

Fixed Expenses

Overhead is constant at $5,000 each month.

Payments to Suppliers
These outlays are concentrated during the heavy production period of March through August.

Cash Disbursements
Cash disbursements includes fixed expenses plus payments to suppliers.

Net Cash Available
Net cash available equals cash available minus cash disbursements.

Bank Loans/Loan Payments
Bank loans/loan payments is the monthly sum necessary to make ending cash equal $20,000. Subtract the ending cash target from cash available. If the sum is positive, the difference may be used as a loan payment; if negative, then this indicates the amount of the draw on your bank line of credit. As may be seen, when cash rolls in during the April to August period when inventory and receivables are mounting, NOEL is drawing heavily on its line.

Precautionary and Speculative Cash Balances

Up until this point, we have concentrated on borrowing to meet everyday transactions demand for money. In practice, businesses also hold money or near money over the course of a year for precautionary and speculative reasons.

Precautionary Balances

Precautionary balances are those held to meet contingencies such as unexpected declines in income or increases in payments. The amount of precautionary balances that a firm might hold depends on (1) management's uncertainty regarding future cash inflows and outflows and (2) the firm's ability to borrow to meet any expected change in cash inflows and outflows. The need to have precautionary balances usually is met by holding interest-bearing deposits or short-term securities.

Speculative Balances

Some firms might hold money or near money temporarily because at the present time they do not wish to invest in plant and equipment or some other asset. These balances are called *speculative balances*. A firm might be saving to buy an asset in the future or because management believes that the asset might be less expensive in the future. Speculative balances almost always are held in interest-bearing deposits or short-term securities.

Summary

Here are the key points in this chapter:

1. Cash is the only asset that is commonly used and generally accepted for goods and services and for the payment of debts.
2. Use a cash budget to manage and plan cash inflows and outflows in your business.
3. Typically a bank line of credit is drawn on to provide short-term cash for short-term purposes.

3

Long-Term Money
for Long-Term Purposes

In Chapter 2 we showed that a firm needs short-term money primarily to finance short-term assets such as inventory and receivables. Planning for these short-term cash needs is accomplished with the use of a cash budget.

In this chapter we will examine long-term uses of funds. By long-term, we mean a period longer than one year. Almost every business has more long-term uses for money than it has available. Therefore, a primary task in this chapter is to learn some basic techniques used to rank long-term projects. The process of planning those expenditures that will benefit a company beyond one year is called *capital budgeting*. We will look at two capital budgeting techniques: (1) the payback method and (2) the net present value method. Finally, we will study The Smith Company from its inception through an expansion phase when it runs into trouble because of inadequate long-term financing.

LONG-TERM NEEDS FOR MONEY

The Basic Principles of Long-Term Financing

Most people own a car in order to get to their job. Cars cost a lot of money. Few people have enough cash saved to pay for a car outright so, if they need a new one, they must borrow the cash to pay for it. They repay the loan over three or four years as they earn the cash from their job that they may keep because they have a car to get to it.

This very simple example illustrates the basic principle of long-term borrowing. *Long-term assets should be financed with long-term funds.* If the benefits from a personal or business asset are spread over a long period, then spread the payments over the same period. Do not finance long-term assets by rolling over 90-day notes at the bank.

Expansion of Plant and Equipment

The most common reason that a firm needs long-term funds is to finance expansion or replacement of plant and equipment. A firm has to have a place to conduct business, and there are varying amounts of equipment necessary to manufacture, distribute, or sell products or services. For any firm, there is an optimal amount of sales and profits that can be generated with a given amount of plant and equipment.

Purchase Another Business

Most business managers have thought at one time or another about buying another business. Such a business could be in a different line, or it could be a competitor. In the first case, the benefits are diversification of sales, profits, and risks. In the second instance, the obvious benefits are expanded sales and, hopefully, increased profits. The benefits of buying another business usually are spread over a long period, hence, long-term financing is needed.

Finance a Permanent Increase in Working Capital

Perhaps the most misunderstood need for long-term funds is the need to finance a permanent increase in working capital (the excess of current assets over current liabilities). Many business managers ordinarily think of all working capital as short-term assets that should be financed with short-term loans. However, what they are confusing is the ordinary seasonal cash cycle similar to that at The NOEL Company in Chapter 2 and a permanently higher *level* of working capital associated with a higher permanent level of sales.

For every firm, there is a definitive and direct relationship between the level of sales and its cash assets, inventory, and receivables. For example, if a firm with sales of $500,000 turns over its inventory two times a year, then its average inventory level is $250,000. If sales levels are expected to climb to $1 million, with the same inventory turnover of two, average inventory must rise to $500,000. If at the old sales level receivables averaged $50,000, then with similar ratios of credit sales and credit terms, the average level of receivables would be expected to increase to $100,000. At the higher sales level, a higher average level of cash is needed to meet weekly expenses, make inventory purchases, and use for other cash needs.

The important point is that the higher level of working capital is a long-term need, not a short-term need. The firm will need the greater amount of cash, inventory, and receivables as long as it has the higher level of sales. These long-term assets should be financed with long-term loans that can be repaid from future profits.

So the question invariably rises: Should I expand the business? This basically means: Should I buy or rent more space and add additional equipment? The question of whether to expand a business depends upon a number of factors. Let's spend just a moment thinking about them.

Expansion of plant and equipment depends first and foremost on whether it is profitable to do so. Therefore, the first task is to determine if expansion will be profitable. We are going to outline two techniques in this chapter to determine the profitability of an investment.

Second, expansion of plant and equipment is made in order to retain customers. This may sound like a strange reason, but often firms are unable to meet the demand for their products or services because poor planning has left them short of capacity. If a firm is unable to meet demand, a competitor may jump in and take advantage of the opportunity. Thus, a share of the market may be permanently lost because of inadequate facilities.

Third, it sometimes is said that "the business that does not grow will die." There is a lot of truth in this statement. In our country, most areas are enjoying increases in population and income. This means that in growth areas generally all businesses have the opportunity to expand sales and profits if they are efficient. Therefore, an important reason for investment expansion is to compete and, hence, to survive.

Replacement and Modernization of Plant and Equipment

Plant and equipment are physical assets that wear out. Use and time are the enemies of physical assets. Old equipment breaks down more frequently, curtailing production and sales. Therefore, from time to time every business is faced with the need to replace and modernize its stock of physical assets. The firm that does not replace equipment periodically is said to be "living off of its assets." This means that the business is overstating profits by not making replacement outlays that would be reflected in additional depreciation expense on the income statement. No firm can do this in the long run and survive. By so doing it is just deceiving itself.

CAPITAL BUDGETING

Nature

One of the best examples of indecision was the mule that starved to death as it stood between two bales of hay trying to make up its mind which bale to eat. Sometimes business managers are confronted with so many investment opportunities that they find it difficult to decide which ones to pursue. In recent years, several financial techniques have been developed to aid managers in choosing among alternative capital outlays. All of these techniques are part of a body of knowledge known as *capital budgeting*, the process of planning those capital outlays that will benefit a company over a time horizon longer than one year. A firm's managers calculate the profitability of each proposed investment outlay and ranks them from highest to lowest profitability. This listing is called a *capital budget*.

Importance

Why is it important to plan future investment outlays? First, by their very nature, plant and equipment are long-lived assets. This means that the expected positive benefits derived from them in the form of increased sales and profits are spread over many years. It also means that if you overestimate expected sales and profits, then you have to find money from other sources to make the payments that you are stuck with for the course of the loan. Thus, capital budgeting is important because it forces you to think and plan ahead so that you minimize the chances of having too much or too little plant and equipment.

Second, and closely related to the first reason, is the importance of capital budgeting in planning the timing of investment outlays. We mentioned earlier the risk of missing out on sales because of inadequate capacity. The capital budgeting process lets you better plan *when* to expand or replace plant and equipment.

Finally, capital budgeting is important because it helps a business plan its borrowing needs. Generally, a creditworthy small business can find adequate long-term financing at local banks or commercial finance companies. However, as a business grows, the arrangement for adequate long-term funds takes more planning and effort. Lenders want more detailed financial information on the business and the projects being financed. Hence, from both a timing dimension and an availability of funds dimension, capital budgeting is essential to the raising of funds.

THE PAYBACK METHOD

How It Works

The simplest capital budgeting technique is to calculate the number of years that it will take for the net cash flow from the new investment to equal the original outlay. In other words, how long will it take to *pay back* the investment?

Estimation of the net cash flows from a project is the most difficult part of the payback method. *Net cash flows* are defined as the net income after taxes plus depreciation that result from a project. How do you estimate net cash flows from a proposed investment? Below is a six-step method to accomplish this task.

Step 1. Estimate the increase in sales that may be expected from the project over its useful life. This involves an estimation of: (a) the number of units that can be sold (Q), (b) the retail price per unit (P), and (c) the useful life. To forecast P and Q, it is necessary to take into account future economic conditions and expected competition and their effects on price, and hence, on the firm's ability to sell. As you can imagine, this is not an easy task.

Step 2. Estimate the increase in costs that may be expected from the project over its useful life. For example, a new branch office will increase personnel expense, utilities, and other direct operating costs. The purchase of a new machine will require maintenance, lubricants, and perhaps special tools. All of the *additional expenses* must be forecast.

Step 2 is the place to take into account those investments that increase net profits by reducing costs. For example, at a store, installation of a TV monitoring system may reduce shoplifting losses. This investment outlay would not increase sales, so no positive benefits would be recorded in Step 1.

Step 3. Subtract the increase in expenses in Step 2 from the increase in sales in Step 1 to determine the change in net operating income before taxes.

Step 4. Multiply net operating income before taxes × (1—the marginal federal and state tax rates) to determine net operating income after taxes. For example, if the firm is in the 46 percent federal marginal tax bracket (that is, it pays federal taxes equal to 46 percent of each additional dollar of net income before taxes), and is in the 7 percent state marginal tax bracket, then the firm will keep 1 − .53, or .47 of each dollar of additional net income before taxes. Make this calculation for each year. Obviously, this step requires a forecast of future tax rates.

Step 5. Estimate the annual depreciation allowance for the project. Depreciation is a noncash expense item in the income statement—an expense for which the firm does not have to pay out cash.

Step 6. For each year add the annual sums found in Steps 4 and 5 to determine the annual net cash flow. After the annual net cash flows are estimated, the payback period is calculated by determining how many years and fractional years it takes to recoup the original outlay. Table 3-1 contains the calculation of the net cash flows and the payback period for a new $10,000 stamping machine for The Essex Company. The payback period is 3.4 years.

A firm using the payback method would calculate the payback period for all projects under consideration. Next, these projects would be ranked by payback period, from shortest to longest. Some firms have a cut-off payback period and will not undertake any projects that have longer payback periods. For example, a manufacturing company with a four-year cut-off period would invest in the stamping machine.

Evaluation of the Payback Method

Advantages

First, companies that use the payback method to evaluate long-term investment projects find this method easy to use, especially on small projects. For larger projects other techniques are used.

Second, for companies that have difficulty borrowing money, the payback method enables these firms to focus on projects with fast payoffs. Presumably, these firms will improve their financial positions quicker with fast payback projects.

Table 3-1. Calculation of Net Cash Flows for a New $10,000 Stamping Machine for The Essex Company.

(1) YEAR	(2) CHANGE IN SALES	(3) CHANGE IN EXPENSES INCLUDING DEPRECIATION	(4) NET OPERATING INCOME BEFORE TAXES (2)-(3)	(5) FEDERAL AND STATE TAXES (53%)	(6) NET INCOME AFTER TAXES (4)-(5)	(7) DEPRECIATION	(8) NET CASH FLOW (6)+(7)
1	$5,000	$2,200	$2,800	$1,484	$1,316	$2,000	$3,316
2	5,000	2,500	2,500	1,325	1,175	2,000	3,175
3	3,000	2,700	300	159	141	2,000	2,141
4	6,000	3,000	3,000	1,590	1,410	2,000	3,410
5	6,000	3,200	2,800	1,484	1,516	2,000	3,516

Payback Period: 3.4 years [3,316 + 3,175 + 2,141 + .4(3,410)] = 10,000.

Finally, some experts argue that net cash flows beyond the three-to-four-year mark are so uncertain anyway that firms might as well use the payback method in lieu of more sophisticated techniques.

Disadvantages

You probably have guessed the major disadvantage of the payback method: it does not recognize returns that may occur after the payback period. Therefore, it is possible for some projects to be overlooked that have higher long-run net cash flows than projects with shorter payback periods. Clearly, these higher net cash flow projects would have a more beneficial effect on the firm.

Closely related to this first disadvantage is that the payback method ignores the *time value of money*. That is, it fails to consider that a dollar payment this year is more valuable than a dollar paid next year. Moreover, a dollar due next year is more valuable than a dollar due three years from now. Therefore, a more accurate evaluation of a proposed project would take into account the present value of all future net cash flows plus depreciation. Such an analytical framework is the net present value method discussed below.

NET PRESENT VALUE METHOD

How It Works

The *net present value (NPV) method* of capital budgeting involves finding the discounted cash value of all future net cash flows, summing these flows, and comparing the total with totals from other projects under consideration. The NPVs for proposed projects are ranked in the capital budget from highest to lowest net present value.

Here are the steps to calculate the NPV for a project.

Step 1. Calculate the annual net cash flow for each year over the life of the project. This is done the same way as for the payback method. In other words, perform Steps 1-5 exactly as you do for the payback method, except be sure to extend it over the life of the project.

Step 2. Estimate the salvage value, if any, for the project. At the end of the useful life for some equipment, it can be sold in the used goods market or as junk. Estimate this value.

Step 3. Determine the marginal cost of capital for the firm. The *marginal cost of capital* is a firm's opportunity cost of investing in the project. That is, it is the interest foregone by investing in a particular project as opposed to investing in another project with similar risks. Let's suppose a business is considering making a "fairly safe investment" in additional production equipment. At the same time, AA corporate bonds, which management deems to be of similar risk, yield 12 percent. Therefore, 12 percent is an appropriate marginal cost of capital to use in discounting future net cash flows from the additional equipment.

Step 4. Using the marginal cost of capital in Step 3, discount all future net cash flows to their present value (PV) and sum them. For those readers not familiar with discounting, here is how to do it with an inexpensive calculator.

First, find the net present value (NPV) of $1 due in one year. The formula for finding this is $NPV = \dfrac{\$1}{(1 + i)^1}$ where i is the marginal cost of capital and the exponent of 1 represents the one year. To find the PV of $1 due in one year using a marginal cost of capital of 12 percent, enter $1 into the calculator and divide it by 1.12. Your answer will be $.893. Looked at another way, $.893 invested for one year at 12 percent will earn $.107 in interest and, hence, principal and interest will equal $1.00 at the end of the year. Since the $.893 is the PV for $1, we can multiply it by any future net cash value to find its PV. Hence, the PV of $1,000 is $893.

Here is the formula to find the PV of $1 due in two years:

$$NPV = \frac{\$1}{(1 + i)^2}$$

To find the PV using a marginal cost of capital of 12 percent, enter $1 in the calculator, divide it by 1.12, and you will get .893 as you did earlier. Now, leave .893 in the calculator and divide it by 1.12. Your answer will be $.797. This sum invested at 12 percent will grow to $1 after 2 years. Since $.797 is the interest factor for $1 at 12 percent for two years, we can multiply .797 times any future net cash flow to find its PV.

Other PVs for $1 at 12 percent or any other interest rate and for other time periods can be calculated in the same manner. Or, you can purchase a set of interest tables and read the values from the appropriate table.

Step 5. Subtract the cost of the project from the sum of the annual PVs to obtain the NPV.

Step 6. Construct a capital budget by listing all NPVs, from highest to lowest, for all projects under consideration.

An Illustration

Table 3-2 contains the NPV's for two projects with identical costs but different patterns of cash flow and different risks. Project A's net cash flow increases over time. On the other hand, Project B's net cash flow declines each year. Moreover, management believes that Project B's risk is higher so a 15 percent discount rate is used to find the PVs.

If we evaluated these projects with the payback method, we would find that Project A has a payback period of 3.72 years, while Project B has a payback period of 2.80 years. Therefore, by the payback method, Project B appears better than Project A. However, using the NPV method, Project A is superior because it

Table 3-2. Calculation of NPV for Projects A and B.

	PROJECT A				PROJECT B		
YEAR	(1) NET CASH FLOW[a]	(2) PV OF $1 @ 12%	(3) PV (1) x (2)	YEAR	(1) NET CASH FLOW[a]	(2) PV OF $1 @ 15%	(3) PV (1) x (2)
1	$1,000	.893	$ 893	1	$2,000	.870	$1,740
2	1,200	.797	956	2	1,800	.756	1,361
3	1,500	.712	1,068	3	1,500	.658	987
4	1,800	.636	1,145	4	1,200	.572	686
5	2,400	.567	1,361	5	1,000	.497	497
Total PV			$5,433	Total PV			$5,271
Less: Cost of Project			− 5,000	Less: Cost of Project			− 5,000
NPV			$ 423	NPV			$ 271

[a] Includes salvage value of $200 in year 5.

has a higher NPV. This fact, along with Project A's apparent lower risk, would have caused us to select Project A over Project B.

Some Important Recommendations

We strongly recommend using the NPV method to evaluate investment projects. The NPV method takes into account: (1) all future net cash flows and (2) the time value of money—both of which are absent from the payback method. Sometimes the payback method is used by large firms to rank small projects. However, for most businesses today, it is easy to compute the NPV for any and all projects. You can buy a calculator for less than $50 that has specific key functions to compute the NPV's. It is unwise not to utilize this technology.

Finally, lenders will be impressed if you can show them your financial evaluation of your potential investments. This has to improve the chances of obtaining the long-term money you need.

THE SMITH COMPANY EXAMPLE

In Chapter 2, we studied The NOEL Company and learned how a cash budget is a vital tool in the management of cash over the an-

Table 3-3. The Smith Company.

	1	2	FYE 1	FYE 2	FYE 3	FYE 4
ASSETS:						
Current Assets:		I. BALANCE SHEET				
Cash	$50,000	$10,000	$9,000	$7,100	$15,300	$ (2,100)
Accounts Receivable			15,000	20,000	20,000	30,000
Inventory		25,000	25,000	30,000	30,000	45,000
Total Current Assets			49,000	57,100	63,300	72,900
Fixed Assets:						
Leasehold Improvements		15,000	15,000	15,000	15,000	25,000
Depreciation Reserve			-2,000	-4,000	-6,000	-9,000
Net Fixed Assets			13,000	11,000	9,000	16,000
Total Assets	50,000	50,000	62,000	68,100	74,300	88,900
LIABILITIES:						
Current Liabilities:						
Due to Banks						
Current Portion L.T. Debt	5,000	5,000	5,000	5,000	5,000	5,000
Accounts Payable			15,000	18,000	18,000	24,000
Total Current Liabilities	5,000	5,000	20,000	23,000	23,000	29,000
Non-Current Liabilities:						
Due Banks	30,000	30,000	25,000	20,000	15,000	10,000
Due Other						
Total Liabilities	35,000	35,000	45,000	45,000	38,000	39,000
STOCKHOLDERS EQUITY						
Common Stock	15,000	15,000	15,000	15,000	15,000	15,000
Retained Earnings			2,000	10,100	21,300	34,900
Net Worth	15,000	15,000	17,000	25,100	36,300	49,900
Total Liabilities & Net Worth	50,000	50,000	62,000	68,100	74,300	88,900

nual cash cycle. In this chapter we have outlined two methods to evaluate long-term investment projects. Also, earlier in this chapter we pointed out that an important long-term need for funds is to finance a permanent increase in working capital.

At this point it would be a good learning experience to have an example that shows a company that:

	1	2	FYE 1	FYE 2	FYE 3	FYE 4
II.		INCOME STATEMENT				
Net Sales	$-0-	$-0-	$100,000	120,000	$130,000	$175,000
Less: COGS			60,000	72,000	78,000	105,000
Gross Profit			40,000	48,000	52,000	70,000
Less: Fixed Expenses			37,600	37,600	37,600	52,600
Net Profit Before Tax			2,400	10,400	14,400	17,400
Less: Taxes			400	2,300	3,200	3,800
Net Profit After Tax			2,000	8,100	11,200	13,600
Retained Earnings Beginning			-0-	2,000	10,100	21,300
Plus: Profit			2,000	8,100	11,200	13,600
Retained Earnings Ending			2,000	10,100	21,300	34,900
III.		CASH BUDGET				
Beginning Cash	$-0-	$50,000	$10,000	$9,000	$7,100	$15,300
Plus:						
Bank Loan	35,000					19,700
Receivables Collections			85,000	115,000	130,000	165,000
Capital Stock	15,000					
Total Receipts	50,000	50,000	95,000	124,000	137,100	200,000
Less:						
Fixed Expenses			35,600	35,600	35,600	49,600
Purchases		25,000	45,000	74,000	78,000	114,000
Fixed Assets		15,000				10,000
Debt Retirement			5,000	5,000	5,000	24,700
Dividends						
Taxes			400	2,300	3,200	3,800
Total Disbursements	-0-	40,000	86,000	116,900	121,800	202,000
Ending Cash	50,000	10,000	9,000	7,100	15,300	(2,100)

The difference between fixed expenses on the income statement and fixed expenses in the cash budget is equal to depreciation charged for each year. No checks are written for depreciation.

- begins business
- operates profitably for a while
- then finds itself in trouble trying to finance long-term needs with a short-term loan

Table 3-3 contains: (1) balance sheets, (2) income statements, and (3) cash budgets for The Smith Company labeled 1,2, and FYE (Fiscal Year End) 1, 2, 3, and 4. The first two show Smith Company getting started while the last four reflect results at the end of the first four years in operation.

Number 1

Balance sheet #1 shows Smith Company's condition right after it raised its initial capital. As you can see, Smith Company began with $50,000 in cash, which includes $35,000 obtained through a seven-year term bank loan and $15,000 from issuance of common stock to the firm's sole owner, Mr. Arnold Smith. Since the bank loan is to be paid over seven years, $5,000 is shown as the current portion of long-term debt, while $30,000 is shown as long-term debt. In other words, Smith Company will pay $5,000 a year as profits come in until the loan is paid in full. The cash budget in #1 shows the sources of cash and ending cash of $50,000.

Number 2

Statement #2 shows that Smith Company used cash to buy $25,000 of inventory and to make $15,000 in leasehold improvements to its rented building in preparation for full operation. These cash outlays are in the cash budget.

FYE 1

Smith Company enjoyed a good first year. Sales covered expenses, and the company made $2,000 net profit. In the cash budget, sources of cash exceeded uses by $9,000, and all looks bright.

FYE 2

More good progress is made this year. Sales increased, and sources of cash exceeded uses by $7,100.

FYE 3

Smith Company looks better than ever. Sales and net profits continued to increase, and cash sources exceeded uses by $15,300.

FYE 4

Early in its fourth year, Smith Company perceived a sharp increase in sales during the year. With memories of the good third year quite vivid, the company sharply stepped up purchases of inventory and made $10,000 in additional leasehold improvements. To help finance these additional assets, it borrowed $19,700 on a six-month bank note that matured at the end of the fiscal year. But notice what happened in the company's cash account; it has a $2,100 overdraft at the bank as all of its end of the month checks cleared. Of course, ending cash in the cash budget reflects the $2,100 overdrawn condition.

What Happened?

The Smith Company experience is typical of many businesses. Smith had a good business plan, and he worked it well until he decided to try to reach for higher sales and profits goals without a plan. During Smith's first three years, sales increased each year, and enough profits were generated to provide funds to make the annual $5,000 loan payment. However, it is a fundamental business relationship that it takes a higher level of assets to generate higher sales and profits. These assets are in the form of higher levels of cash, inventory, receivables, and perhaps leasehold improvements as in Smith's case. These assets must be purchased with cash from some source.

What Should Smith Have Done?

When Smith decided to expand, he should have made up a new cash budget plan for his business. He should have realized that each of his additional assets represented a long-term commitment that must be paid for out of long-term profits. Hence, Smith should have gone back to his lender with his plan and borrowed new long-term money to finance his needs. If Smith had reworked the original $35,000 loan back from $15,000 (where the long-term portion was at the end of FYE 3) to $25,000 with $5,000 payments for five more years, he would not be in trouble at FYE 4. In fact, he would have $7,900 in the bank and be in great shape.

Here's how! Smith increased inventory by $15,000, receivables by $10,000, and leasehold improvements by $10,000 for a total of $35,000 expansion in assets. Yet at FYE 3, Smith had the following cash flow available or anticipated:

Cash account at FYE 3	$15,300
Anticipated increase in trade credit	
(accounts payable) during FYE 4	6,000
Depreciation	3,000
Net profit	13,600
Bank loan payment	- 5,000
Total cash available from internal sources	$32,900
Cash needs	- 35,000
Cash deficit	-$ 2,100

If he had forecast the increase in trade credit and net profit precisely, he still would have been $2,100 in the hole in his cash account. However, look at Smith's condition with a $10,000 increase in his bank term loan:

Total cash from internal sources	$32,900
Cash from increase in bank loan	10,000
Total cash available	$42,900
Cash needs	35,000
Ending cash	$ 7,900

SUMMARY

Here are the key points in this chapter:

1. Investment in long-term assets requires careful planning because mistakes of overcapacity or undercapacity can be costly for years to come.
2. Capital budgeting is the process of planning expenditures over a long period of time.

3. The payback method of capital budgeting is quick and easy, but it does not take into account all future net cash flows or the time value of money.
4. The NPV method of capital budgeting generally is considered the best method to use because it takes into account all future net cash flows and the time value of money.
5. Rank all proposed investment projects by NPV, from highest to lowest, and undertake those with the highest NPV.
6. Trying to finance long-term needs with short-term borrowing usually leads to cash shortages.

4

Where to Find the Money You Need

After you have determined how much short-term and/or long-term money you need, the next step is to find a lender who will make you a loan. There are many lending institutions and sources of money in the marketplace. During the course of a normal week, you probably will see TV commercials extolling the benefits from dealing with America's "Full Service Banks" or telling you how easy it is to borrow from "XYZ Finance Company." One finance company's slogan is, "We're proud to lend you money." This kind of attitude makes you feel so good that you may want to jump out of your chair and rush down to get some money.

The goal in this chapter is to outline for you the major sources of business loans. Remember: "Knowing how to fish involves knowing primarily *where* to fish." Further, the more you know about the nature of the lending institutions or companies that you wish to borrow from, the better your chances of getting the money you need. Knowledge about the potential lender has a spillover effect. The lender reasons that if you know so much about his firm, you must be knowledgeable about how to run your own business.

COMMERCIAL BANKS

Commercial banks are the primary source of money for small businesses. The word "commercial" stems from the fact that since the days of the great Italian banking houses in Florence in the fifteenth and sixteenth centuries, banks have provided the lion's share of the credit to finance commerce. Banks want to make good, sound business loans, so these institutions must be among the first sources of money to consider.

What is a Bank?

Essentially, a *bank* is an institution that obtains funds by issuing common stock, accepting demand and savings deposits, and borrowing from other lenders and which, in turn, creates *credit* (the obligation to repay money in the future) as it makes loans and purchases investment securities. There are over 14,000 banks in America. These banks also operate 34,000 branches, thus making 48,000 total banking offices. Banks range in size from $1-2 million in assets to over $100 billion for Bank of America in California and Citibank in New York.

Banks are chartered by both the federal and state governments. The federal government, through the Office of the Comptroller in the Treasury Department, charters national banks. Each state has an agency that charters state banks. All national banks must have the word "national" in the title such as, for example, First National Bank. As far as safety and soundness, all banks are closely regulated, so you really do not have to be concerned with whether you borrow from a national or state bank. Virtually all banks in America have their depositors insured by the Federal Deposit Insurance Corporation (FDIC) for an amount up to $100,000. All national banks are insured banks. If you have any doubt about other banks, look for the FDIC seal. It must be displayed in a prominent place at the bank.

When it comes to finding a bank with which to do business, the fact that there are a large number of banking offices in the nation is a little misleading. Banks at the other end of the country obviously are not viable sources of money to you. In your quest for money, you basically are limited to the banks in your community. Banks outside of this area are not anxious to lend you money because of the higher costs of checking your credit and of collecting the loan if you default. Moreover, most banks will not lend to you unless you have a checking or savings account with them. Out-oftown banks know that you are not likely to keep meaningful deposits with them because it is too costly in both time and expense. It is best to confine your search for a bank source of funds to your local area. You probably have accounts with them now which is a positive factor when you apply for a loan.

What kinds of business loans do banks make? Answer: just about any kind that you can think of. Bank business loans may be classified as: (1) short-term loans or (2) term loans. A *short-term loan* has a maturity or less than a year, while a *term loan* has a maturity of one year or more.

Short-Term Bank Loans

Short-term loans basically are working capital loans. As such they are for meeting payrolls, purchasing inventory, carrying accounts receivable, paying taxes, paying insurance premiums, or any short-term cash need. Short-term money may be obtained under several types of lending arrangements: (1) line of credit, (2) revolving credit agreement, and (3) individual transaction loans.

Line of Credit

A typical way of meeting short-term money needs is by borrowing on a *line of credit* which is an informal agreement whereby a bank extends to a customer the privilege to borrow up to some maximum amount at any time during a specified period, usually a year. To obtain a line of credit, you would submit your personal and business' statement of condition and income statement for evaluation as part of a loan request. If the bank approves a line of credit for your business, the bank will write you a letter that specifies the amount of credit under the line, the expiration date, the interest rate, and any other terms and conditions such as collateral or security and perhaps a 10 percent compensating balance requirement. For example, if your line of credit is $50,000, then you must keep an average of $5,000 in your checking account. If you have this much on deposit when you apply for credit, then there is no problem. In addition you may negotiate with your banker whether or not business time or savings deposits meet the compensating balance requirements. When you receive the letter with the bank's commitment to a line of credit, it is a good idea to acknowledge the letter in writing. Although a bank may not be legally bound to honor such commitments, they usually do because customers who can obtain a line of credit ordinarily are highly valuable to the bank and are good credit risks.

The primary advantage of a line of credit is that you do not have to reapply for a loan every time funds are needed. During the period that the line is effective, you can borrow funds when you need them simply by seeing your loan officer, signing a note, and asking him to credit your account with the necessary amount. While the line is in effect, you can reduce your interest costs by making payments on the loan amount outstanding.

Revolving Credit Agreement.
A *revolving credit agreement* is a binding legal commitment by a bank to allow a customer to borrow up to some maximum limit at any time during a specified period, usually two or three years. Each party signs a contract that contains the terms of the commitment including any security or collateral that must be pledged. In the agreement there may be *affirmative covenants* which are promises by the borrower to perform certain actions either automatically or at the request of the bank, for example by keeping all properties in good repair, paying promptly all taxes, maintaining a minimum net working capital, or maintaining a minimum net worth. Also in the agreement there may be *negative covenants* which are promises by the borrowing firm that it will not perform certain actions without the bank's prior written consent. Examples of negative covenants placed on a firm include promises not to purchase or retire any of its capital stock, not to change the general nature of its business, and not to pay dividends in excess of some specified percentage of after-tax profit. For the

right to borrow under a revolving credit, you should expect to pay a *commitment fee* of about one-half of one percent of the unused portion of the revolving credit outstanding.

Individual Transaction Loans

Sometimes borrowers do not a want a line of credit or revolving credit agreement, but prefer to borrow only on an *individual transaction basis* or whenever an opportunity presents itself. For example, the owner of a laundromat chain may wish to borrow only when he makes periodic purchases of new washing machines and dryers. A retail furniture dealer might have an opportunity to buy the inventory of a bankrupt store at a reduced price. He might obtain the funds on a short-term note and, as the furniture is sold, repay the debt. Usually individual transaction loans are secured by the item necessitating the loan and, as such, take on the name of the item financed. *Inventory loans, accounts receivable loans,* and *equipment loans* are good examples of these kinds of credits.

Advantages of Short-Term Bank Loans

Lower interest rates. Bank interest rates on business loans typically are lower than those charged by commercial finance companies. Because finance companies obtain most of their funds from banks and through the money market, they must charge a rate sufficiently high to cover the cost of funds and administrative costs and produce a profit.

Unsecured loans. An important advantage to creditworthy businesses of borrowing from a bank is that many times the funds can be obtained on an unsecured basis. However, a bank may require that you agree not to pledge any assets of your business to any other lender while the bank loan is outstanding. Such an arrangement is called a *negative pledge* agreement.

Reliable source of funds during credit crunches. During certain periods of the business cycle, the demand for credit becomes so great in relation to the amount available that many large businesses find it difficult to sell commercial paper[1] in the market-place. In addition, many small to medium-sized firms may be unable to obtain adequate loans from commercial finance companies who themselves find it difficult to borrow from banks or in the open market. In a credit crunch, banks generally have a great deal more flexibility in obtaining funds and hence are better able to meet the credit needs of their customers. Moreover, bankers feel an obligation to take care of their good customers during periods of tight credit and will try to find a way to obtain the necessary funds.

Advice of experienced business counselors. In the course of making business loans, bank loan officers become familiar with financial problems that are common to all businesses. As you work out the details of a loan, the bank officer can utilize his experience to advise and counsel you on financial matters so that you will not repeat the mistakes of others. Also, your loan officer can share with you knowledge about expected developments in the economy and perhaps tell you about potential customers for your business.

Availability of other services. Besides serving as a source of funds, banks offer under one roof a variety of other services such as checking and savings accounts, lockbox collection services, wire transfers of funds, mortgage loans, trust services, foreign exchange, and data processing.

Bank Term Loans

As you recall, bank term loans have a maturity of one year or longer. Typical maturities are three to five years, but a few large loans extend to 15 years. It was pointed out in Chapter 3 that you should finance long-term assets with long-term loans. Two primary uses of bank term loans are: (1) to purchase a business and (2) to purchase additional plant and equipment for a going con-

---

[1]*Commercial paper* represents short-term promissory notes sold in the money market by prime-rated businesses.

cern. Another important use of term loans is to finance a permanent increase in working capital needed support a higher level of
sales.

Advantages of Bank Term Loans

Bank term loans have a number of advantages over other means
of long-term financing.

Flexibility. First, bank term loans are very flexible. Unlike a bond
issue for which payments must be made precisely in accordance
with a prearranged schedule, bank term loans may be paid any
number of ways. For example, there may be small quarterly in-
stallments with a large annual payment or straight monthly payments or annual payments. Any reasonable schedule can be ac-
commodated. If, for some reason, a firm cannot meet its payment
schedule, the bank can restructure the schedule quite easily, provided the request is reasonable from a credit standpoint.

Speed. Unlike a public offering of bonds or stock which often
takes months to arrange, a bank term loan can be obtained in a
matter of several days or a few weeks at most.

Lower cost. Given the registration and underwriting fees involved
with a public offering, the overall cost of a bank loan probably
will be lower. Moreover, the interest rate on a term loan can be ne-
gotiated to fluctuate with the prime rate, and this fact may produce a lower average cost over the life of the loan. Finally, the
term loan arrangement might permit payment ahead of schedule
thereby reducing the overall cost of funds.

Financial counseling. Sometimes an overlooked advantage of obtaining funds under a bank term loan is the financial counseling
available to a business from the bank. In the evaluation of a loan
request, the bank's credit analysts and loan officers must become
familar with all facets of the firm's operations. Because the officers have had broad experience in arranging loans for many
other firms, perhaps in the same industry, the borrowing firm
stands to benefit greatly from the advice, counsel, and indepen-

dent evaluation of the firm's operations and plans offered by them.

Disadvantages of Bank Term Loans

In some situations there are disadvantages from borrowing term money from a bank. First, the affirmative and negative covenants of a loan agreement limit the firm's latitude of operations and hence are considered by most business borrowers as drawbacks to term loans. Second, maturities allowed under term loans may not be as long as some firms might prefer. Finally, for some large borrowers, a bank's legal lending limit may be a drawback to term lending. However, this handicap usually is overcome through the use of a *participation loan* in which several banks agree to lend various portions of the amount required.

Joint Lending

In some instances it will be appropriate for a bank to participate with specialized lenders to help you get the money you need. For example, while banks compete with commercial finance companies, they may participate in loans with them allowing the finance company to manage the account from an operational and control point of view with the bank furnishing a substantial portion of the dollars for loan funds.

Interest on Bank Loans

The specific interest charge on a bank business loan will depend on a number of factors including the general level of interest rates, the riskiness of the loan, the size of the loan, the section of the country where the loan is made, and whether the loan is secured or unsecured.

The general level of interest rates is determined in the financial markets primarily by Federal Reserve monetary policy and the demand for credit. A good measure of the general level of interest rates is the *prime rate*, the rate charged by banks for short-term loans of the highest credit quality. When GMAC borrows from banks to finance car loans, it pays the prime rate. In recent years the prime rate has ranged from 5-21.5 percent.

Most growing businesses have to pay an interest rate higher than the prime rate because of the greater risk involved. However, the prime rate serves as the base rate in setting all interest rates. For example, if your business is relatively new with a short track record, the bank might set the rate at prime plus two points for a risk premium. Thus, if the prime rate is 10 percent, you would pay 12 percent for the money. Generally, small businesses pay from one-half to five points above prime for bank loans. If your net income is growing, if your level of debt-to-equity capital is reasonable, if you have good deposit balances with the bank, and if your financial house is otherwise in order, then you can bargain for a lower risk premium. In other words, as your record of performance in the marketplace improves and your track record lengthens, let your banker know that you feel that the risk involved with your credit has diminished and therefore you may deserve a lower interest rate.

Regardless of financial condition, non-prime rate borrowers on the West Coast should expect to pay slightly higher rates above prime because banks there tend to have a higher cost of funds and because the demand for credit is greater in this growing area.

Finally, many borrowers ask: Should I not get a lower interest rate if my loan is secured? The answer generally is no because of the fact that if a bank asks for security there is an indication that the loan appears to be more risky. Also, secured loans are more costly to put on the bank's books because of the greater amount of paperwork involved.

FINANCE COMPANIES

Let's turn now to finance companies which rank as the second largest source of business loans. The finance company industry is diverse so it would be helpful to spend a moment learning to identify the kinds of finance companies that you should consider as sources of funds.

Nature and Types

A *finance company* simply is a business that borrows funds in the money and capital markets and lends these dollars at a higher rate to individuals and businesses. Below is an outline of the different types of finance companies.

Types of Finance Companies	Examples
I. Consumer Finance Companies	
A. Captive sales finance companies	GMAC, Ford Motor Credit, Chrysler Financial
B. Personal finance companies	Beneficial Finance Company, Person-to-Person Financial Center
II. Commercial Finance Companies	
A. Captive	General Electric Credit Corporation (GECC), Westinghouse Credit
B. Independent	CIT Corporation, Commercial Credit, Walter E. Heller International Corporation, James Talcott

As the name implies, *consumer finance companies* lend primarily to people to finance the purchase of all kinds of goods and services. These companies may be classified as *captive sales finance companies* such as GMAC, which primarily finances the purchase of new cars bought from GM dealers. GMAC is considered a *captive* company because it is owned by GM and exists basically to serve the interests of the parent company.

Personal finance companies are in virtually every city in America. They have offices in most large shopping centers, so they are as convenient as the nearest bank branch. Personal finance companies make secured loans to individuals for almost any purpose imaginable, including starting a business. However, personal finance companies generally are not going to lend you more than $7,500 and the rate charged can be high.

Commercial finance companies are in practically every city with a population of 50,000 or more and are in business to make loans to businesses. However, their representatives travel throughout the country looking for loans in any size city. Commercial finance companies are either captive or independent. Captive companies either are *nondiversified* because they finance only sales of the product of the parent manufacturing company or clients of the parent, or they are *diversified* because, in addition to financing products, they make loans to any qualified business borrower. GECC is a good illustration of a captive company that has branched out into all types of business lending.

Besides the captive companies, there are large *independent* commercial finance companies that make all types of business loans. Get the phone book and look up "Finance Companies" in the yellow pages. In larger cities, you will see offices for such giants as CIT Corporation, Commercial Credit, Walter E. Heller International Corporation, and James Talcott. In their ads, these companies state the kinds of loans that they make. For example, here is the list from a CIT Corporation ad:

- industrial financing of income producing machinery and equipment
- working capital loans
- accounts receivable financing
- inventory financing

In the first category, CIT finances machinery and equipment for businesses on a monthly installment basis. Loan maturities generally match the useful life of the equipment which usually is four to seven years. Interest rates on these loans are competitive with those offered by banks.

Working capital loans, of course, are the same short-term loans that we discussed in Chapter 2. All of these loans are secured and the rate charged generally will be higher than the bank rate.

Accounts receivable financing and inventory financing are the most typical loans made by commercial finance companies. Let's look at these more closely.

Accounts Receivable Financing

Usually as sales grow, a business' accounts receivable increase also. This means that more of a company's cash assets become tied up in debts and are not available to purchase additional inventory, meet payrolls, or use for any other purposes. *An increase in receivables usually is the primary reason that a business becomes squeezed for cash.* There are two ways out of this predicament: (1) make more cash sales or (2) use receivables as collateral for a loan.

Under an accounts receivable loan agreement the borrower pledges or assigns all of his receivables as security for the loan. Typically, the finance company or bank will lend an amount equal to 75–80 percent of the amount of eligible outstanding receivables (those current within 90 days). The borrower signs an agreement pledging its receivables to the lender and advances are made as required as long as specifications in the agreement are met. As draws are made, the borrower certifies that excess collateral (receivables) is available and loans against the free collateral can be made. The borrower still has the responsibility for collection of the receivables, but the borrower must remit collected funds promptly to the finance company or bank. Interest charges are calculated daily, so the borrower can minimize his interest costs by paying promptly.

Accounts receivable financing is high-cost financing because the lender must charge a higher rate because of the added risk and paperwork involved. There is greater risk because the business that has to resort to pledging receivables for cash has a liquidity problem. However, for new businesses and those experiencing rapid growth, accounts receivable financing with a commercial finance company or a bank can make the difference between survival and bankruptcy.

Inventory Financing

A significant percentage of a business' assets usually are tied up in inventory. The firm without adequate cash must rely on commercial finance companies or banks to finance this inventory. Under typical inventory financing arrangements, the bank takes a lien on or title to the goods which may be: (1) sitting on the borrower's floor, (2) in a secure area on the borrower's premises under control of a bonded warehouseman employed by a professional warehouse company, or (3) in a bonded warehouse off-premises.

In the first case above, which is commonly known as *floor planning,* goods remain in the possession of the borrower, title is with the lender, and the borrower must remit payment as goods are sold. To prevent fraud in reporting goods sold, the lender must check inventory each month. Floor planning is used primarily for big-ticket items such as cars and appliances.

Because of the opportunities for fraud, a number of companies provide bonded warehouse services either on- or off-premises. If the goods are on the premises, the borrower will construct a cage to hold the merchandise. An outside bonded warehouseman has control over the goods for the lender and releases it to the borrower after obtaining a proper receipt and assurance that the lender will be paid as per the agreement. An off-premises bonded warehouse arrangement works the same way except the warehouse company has goods for many firms under its control.

As you may have guessed, because of greater risk, paperwork and time, the interest cost for inventory financing at either a commercial finance company or bank is much higher than on a straight unsecured bank working capital loan. This added cost is an added incentive for businessmen to have adequate capital, collect receivables promptly, and keep a tight rein on inventory.

Factoring

Closely related to accounts receivables financing is *factoring,* which involves the sale of receivables to a factoring company which collects them. The factor charges service charges and interest on funds remitted prior to the time of actual collection of the receivables.

An important advantage of factoring receivables is that a business may eliminate its credit and collection department and reduce bookkeeping and credit personnel. Factoring services are utilized extensively by carpet and furniture manufacturers. However, in recent years all kinds of businesses that generate receivables have used the services of a factor. Most large banks have a factoring department or own a factoring subsidiary. If you think that a factor might be of service to your business, ask your banker for a reference. However, weigh carefully the benefits and the costs. If your net margin on sales is four percent, a two percent factor service charge takes a big chunk out of profits.

VENDORS AND TRADE CREDIT

Every business uses trade credit. In our economy buyers usually are not required to pay for goods upon delivery but are allowed a short time before payment is due. During the period between delivery and payment, the buyer is using *trade credit*. This obligation is recorded on the liability side of the balance sheet under "accounts payable."

There are two basic types of trade credit: (1) open account and (2) notes payable. Under the more typical open account method, the buyer accepts delivery and pays for the goods as per the terms stated on the invoice. Under the notes payable method, the buyer signs a note which is a formal acknowledgement of the debt.

In the use of trade credit, it is important to pay close attention to the *terms of sale* stated on the invoice. Of course, if the invoice says C.O.D. (cash on delivery) or C.B.D. (cash before delivery), there is no credit. If the terms are net 30, this means that full payment is expected in 30 days. Some invoices state net 10, meaning full payment is due in 10 days. In these cases, the buyer receives credit at no interest cost for 30 and 10 days, respectively. On the other hand, if the terms of sale are 2/10, net 30, the buyer receives a 2 percent cash discount if the invoice is paid within 10 days, but the full amount is due within 30 days. If the buyer does not take the cash discount, he loses interest at a very high annual rate. For example, suppose that you had a $1,000 invoice that stated 2/10, net 30. If the discount was not taken, the firm in effect paid $20 for the use of $980 over 20 days. Based on a 360-day year to facilitate the calculation, the annual interest cost is:

$$\frac{20}{980} \times \frac{360}{20} = 36.7 \text{ percent.}$$

The business could have borrowed from the bank or a commercial finance company at a much lower rate, taken the cash discount, and saved a lot of interest. You should be able to see why it is smart to have enough cash or credit to take all the cash discounts offered. The business with a four percent pretax margin on sales that takes a two percent cash discount on all purchases would boost profits considerably.

We recommend full utilization of trade credit and that you take all cash discounts. The chief advantage of trade credit is that it is readily available. Also, it increases automatically as the need increases. As your inventory requirements increase, so does the trade credit to finance them. However, trade credit is very short-term, with typical terms ranging from 10–60 days. Do not abuse the trade credit privilege by being late with payments because suppliers could shift to a C.O.D. or C.B.D. arrangement.

LEASING COMPANIES

Lease financing has become very popular over the last 25 years. Today, a business can lease almost anything. This includes items for everyday use such as automobiles, office copiers and machines, computers, furniture, and even the land and building where the business is situated. In addition, a business can lease special purpose items such as cranes, air compressors, large trucks, and all types of tools. Turn to "Leasing" in the yellow pages of the phone book, and you will see a list of leasing companies and examples of what you can lease. Many of the companies listed are subsidiaries of large, recognized corporations or commercial finance companies that also provide leasing services.

Advantages of Leasing

Obviously, instead of leasing a piece of equipment, you could borrow the money from a bank or finance company and buy the item outright. What, then, are the advantages of leasing?

100 Percent Financing

Many growing businesses probably have "borrowed up to their limit" at their bank and/or commercial finance company. This may not be a valid assumption, but many businessmen may be reluctant to make further inquiry at their major lender. Therefore, when a new piece of equipment is needed, leasing appears to be the only alternative. A primary advantage of leasing is that usually a business can obtain 100 percent financing for the item. In other words, ordinarily no down payment is necessary. Just sign the lease agreement and start using the item.

Flexibility

Leasing enables a business to obtain the use of equipment as it is needed. A new business might start up fully equipped, but from this point on, the typical case is for equipment to be added on an "as needed" basis. Some businessmen believe that leasing offers a more flexible way to acquire the use of equipment during strong growth phases of a company.

Tax Advantages

Lease payments are deductible as a business expense. On the other hand, if you own the item, depreciation is a deductible expense, and you will receive an investment tax credit. However, some businesses are unable to take full advantage of accelerated depreciation or the investment tax credit. Therefore, under these conditions leasing offers a tax advantage. A second tax advantage stems from the ability to deduct lease payments where land is involved. Payments for the direct purchase of land are not deductible, of course. Therefore, by leasing a building site, a business can obtain a larger deduction than if it deducted interest on the mortgage and only depreciation on the building.

Disadvantages of Leasing

Higher Interest Cost

Leasing consultants point out that in practically all cases, interest costs in leasing are higher than those to carry an equivalent amount of debt to finance the direct purchase of an item.[2] This is just a cost that some firms must bear because of the inability (valid or invalid) to borrow.

Possible Loss of Residual/Salvage Value

At the end of the lease period, the leasee usually has the right to purchase the item for a nominal sum such as $1 or $10. However, if the lease contract specifies the leasee may buy the item only at fair market value and over the lease period inflation has sharply increased replacement value, then fair market value may be a significant percentage of original cost. In this case, the leasee would have been in a much better position owning the asset instead of leasing. Hence, you should inquire how residual values are handled and try to obtain the option to buy the asset at a low residual value.

INDIVIDUALS

An important source of money for new and growing businesses is individuals. Many people who have a great idea for a business frequently borrow from relatives, friends, or wealthy individuals who have money to lend. The borrower either gives the lender a note for the money or stock in the business. Of course, just as with a bank loan, notes to individuals can be either secured or unsecured. With respect to the interest rate, usury laws still apply to these transactions, so do not let the lender hold you up for an exorbitant rate.

---

[2]If the full cost of the asset is amortized over the lease period, then the interest cost is the rate of discount (interest) that will make the sum of the present values of the lease payments equal to the cost of the asset.

GOVERNMENT PROGRAMS

In addition to the above sources of loans, if you meet certain criteria there are a number of government programs that directly or indirectly can assist you in borrowing the money you need. Many government programs support lenders by making sources of funds available to them. For example, Export-Import Bank of the United States will allow lenders to discount loans that have its guarantee thus providing a liquidity feature that affords the lender flexibility in funding additional loans.

Government programs exist on the federal, state, and local levels. Federal agencies with such programs include The Small Business Administration (SBA), The Farmers Home Administration (FMHA), and the Economic Development Administration. At the state and local level, a number of business development corporations exist to help obtain funds for qualifying businesses.

In general, government programs are designed to stimulate economic development and take the form of either direct loans or guarantees to conventional lenders. Direct loans usually are made under the aegis of specialized lending situations. For instance, Federal Land Banks make long-term loans to farmers, Federal Intermediate Credit Banks make intermediate-term loans for agricultural purposes to Production Credit Associations, and Banks for Cooperatives make direct loans to farm-related co-ops.

Guaranteed loans are made by conventional lenders who for some reason do not want to make the entire loan applied for. Probably best known are the SBA and the FMHA commercial and industrial loan guarantee programs. Under these programs the conventional lender's loan is guaranteed up to 90 percent and his risk commensurately reduced. Both of these agencies require that the borrower make conventional applications and be turned down prior to their consideration of an application for guarantee. Normally conventional lenders such as commercial banks are very familiar with government programs and if they cannot handle your credit request they can steer you to the proper agency for assistance.

SUMMARY

Here are the key points in this chapter:

1. Commercial banks are the primary source of money for small businesses. Banks can make just about any kind of loan that you can think of.
2. A line of credit, a revolving credit agreement, and individual transaction loans are the primary borrowing arrangements at banks.
3. Commercial finance companies are important sources of money to businesses through accounts receivable, inventory, working capital, and equipment loans.
4. Make full utilization of trade credit but take all cash discounts.
5. Leasing offers several advantages: 100 percent financing, flexibility, and tax breaks. However, leasing tends to involve higher interest costs and a possible loss of residual/salvage values.
6. There are some specialized government programs that involve loan guarantees or direct loans to qualifying individuals or businesses. Normally, conventional lenders are familiar with government programs and if they cannot handle your request they can steer you to the proper agency for assistance.

5

How to Apply for the Money You Need

Chapter 4 was concerned with *WHERE* to find the money you need. Now let's look at *HOW* to apply for a loan. In the last chapter, we said "knowing how to fish involves knowing primarily *where* to fish." But, "once you find the right fishing hole, you still have to bait the hook."

Our goals in this chapter are to learn: (1) how to select an appropriate lender, (2) the three questions that every lender asks, (3) the specific information that you must provide the lender, (4) how to prepare for the loan interview, and (5) what experts are available to help you apply for the money you need.

SELECTION OF A LENDER

How to apply for a loan depends mostly on *where* you apply for a loan. This depends in part on the purpose of the loan. In most cases, you should begin your search for funds at a commercial bank. Banks are by far the largest financial institution and as such provide the vast majority of the funds to finance America's businesses. Second, most banks are general purpose lenders that can take care of just about any credit need that a business might have. Third, the cost of a bank loan ordinarily will be lower than the cost of funds obtained at other lenders. Finally, a knowledgeable and professional banker can serve as an objective evaluator of your money needs and your ability to repay the money. If he thinks your request is "not bankable," he should be able to refer you to nonbank lenders that may be able to help you.

Many small banks do not have the specially trained personnel needed to make certain kinds of loans. For example, typically small banks do not offer leasing agreements, accounts receivable financing, factoring, or long-term mortgage credit. However, most bankers at large or small institutions are well-informed about which lenders in the community provide these kinds of financing. Moreover, since the banker may be financing these specialized lending companies, he is in a position to "make a phone call" to arrange an appointment for you.

In a nutshell, here are the steps that we suggest that you take in your selection of a lender:

1. If you have a banker that has worked with you before, see him first.
2. If you do not have a banker that has worked with you previously, make a list of the banks that are convenient to you. Call several friends in business and ask them to suggest an experienced banker that understands business needs.
3. After you have finished this book and have a clear idea of how much money you need, why you need it, how you are going to pay it back, and are prepared for the loan interview, then go see your banker or one that perhaps a friend has recommended.
4. If the banker cannot assist you, ask him to recommend a lender who might and go to see him. Your banker may recommend a commercial finance company to handle your working capital needs or a leasing company if leasing appears to be the way to go.

We wish to make it very clear that our recommendation that you start your search for funds at a bank is not based on any bias or prejudice against other lenders. It is based on generally accepted knowledge that banks are best suited to handle most of your credit needs. Other lenders such as commercial finance companies are set up to handle more risky loans or specialized credits such as receivables financing, factoring, or leasing.

Regardless of which lender you choose, all will request much the same financial and credit information about your business. In the case of receivables or inventory financing, you will have to provide detailed data about the receivables or inventory. Let's turn now to the questions that every lender will ask you.

THREE QUESTIONS THAT EVERY LENDER ASKS

Anybody who has ever borrowed money knows that a loan interview can be an awkward situation. Here you are with your hat in your hand feeling that you are at the mercy of the lender and that you do not like having to "bare your soul" to the lender. He has the money and you do not. He is sitting behind an imposing desk, and you are sitting on the edge of an unfamiliar chair. However, try not to think of the loan interview as an inquisition, but as a straight business deal much like you do every day with one of your customers. After all, you are going to pay interest and perhaps fees on the borrowed money. Lending money is a business that has an income statement. The lender needs you just as much as you need him. So relax! The questions that we shall consider below are the same questions that you would ask if you were lending money. In fact, if your children have ever asked you for more money than their allowance, you probably asked them the same three questions.

What is the Purpose of the Loan?

The first question right off the top of the deck is: What is the purpose of the loan or why do you want the money? The primary purpose of this question is to determine the income creation potential and risk exposure of the money requested. People request loans for every conceivable purpose, some of which have a high probability of loss attached to them. For example, the authors have seen or heard of loan requests from the following: (1) a business with a negative net worth (liabilities exceed assets), (2) a businessman who needed funds and was offering a fifth mortgage on his property, and (3) quite typically, a business with a string of judgments against it on the courthouse records. Every experienced lender has stories about "his most incredible" loan requests.

So, it is a very legitimate question to ask you why you want the money. It may be that the lender has special information about business conditions or potential competitors for your product that you do not have. It could be that this information has an important bearing on your need for funds. An often overlooked function of a lender is to "keep the borrower out of trouble." When the purpose of your loan and other details about your loan request are revealed, the lender may be doing you a big favor by declining the loan request if he thinks that the money cannot be used profitably in your business and that you may have difficulty paying it back.

Answer the loan purpose question honestly. If it is a working capital loan to smooth out your cash cycle, tell the lender this. If it is to buy equipment, another business, or finance a permanent increase in working capital, lay the request on the table.

Do not tell the lender you need money for one purpose when you really intend to use the money for another purpose like investing in the stock market, buying land as a speculation, repaying another loan that you are delinquent on, or taking a trip to Europe. Remember, it is against the law to use fraud to obtain a loan, so tell the truth. If you need money to repay another loan, tell the lender the whole story. He has heard it before.

How Much Money Do You Need?

When the lender asks you how much money you need, do not hem and haw; tell him and then pull out your cash budget if you need a working capital loan, or pull out your capital budget and NPV calculations if it is a long-term project. Believe us, if you pull out these documents the lender's eyes may blink in amazement or his jaw will drop or, if he is leaning back in a chair, he just may fall out. To be organized and precise at this crucial point in the loan interview is vitally important and will pay dividends.

With respect to short-term money for short-term purposes, your cash budget will reveal the maximum amount that you need on a line of credit over the coming year and cash cycle. Hand the cash budget to the loan officer, then be quiet and let him study it. He may ask you to explain the basis for your sales projections and to comment on your policy with respect to receivables collections.

If you seek long-term money for long-term purposes, hand over NPV calculations to the loan officer for his review. His questions here may pertain to the cost of the project, how you estimated the net cash flow, and how you chose the interest rate for the cost of capital. Explain all of this to him.

What are the Sources of Repayment?

As the loan officer completes his review of the documents that substantiate the amount requested, the logical final question is where are you going to get the cash to repay the loan? There are only three sources of cash to repay any loan:

1. *Conversion of assets*—the sale of fixed assets and/or the conversion of inventory into receivables and receivables into cash.
2. *Profits*—those available after payment of expenses and maturing liabilities.
3. *Borrowing cash from another source.*

Conversion of inventory and receivables into cash is the primary source of repayment of short-term loans for short-term purposes. Therefore, the lender will want to look closely at your past and *pro forma* (estimated) balance sheets to evaluate the firm's liquidity, which is defined as a firm's ability to pay its obligations. This is done by looking at the following *liquidity ratios:*

1. Current Ratio $= \dfrac{\text{current assets}}{\text{current liabilities}}$

2. Acid Test or Quick Ratio $= \dfrac{\text{current assets - inventories}}{\text{current liabilities}}$

3. Average Collection Period Ratio $= \dfrac{\text{receivables x 360}}{\text{annual credit sales}}$

4. Inventory Turnover Ratio $= \dfrac{\text{cost of goods sold}}{\text{average inventory}}$

All of these ratios measure how well a company can convert assets into cash in order to repay short-term debt.

Profits are the primary source of cash to repay long-term loans. In other words, your business must be able to take the proceeds of a loan and use them so effectively in the business that profits generated from the project and other operations over the life of the loan are adequate to repay the debt.

To evaluate your ability to generate profits, the loan officer will want to analyze your past and *pro forma* income statements and look specifically at the following *profitability ratios:*

1. Gross Profit Margin $= \dfrac{\text{sales - cost of goods sold}}{\text{sales}}$

2. Net Profit Margin $= \dfrac{\text{net profit}}{\text{sales}}$

3. Rate of Return on Owners' Equity $= \dfrac{\text{net profit}}{\text{owners' equity}}$

4. Rate of Return on Assets $= \dfrac{\text{net profit}}{\text{total assets - intangible assets}}$

He also may wish to obtain a quantitative measure of the firm's ability to pay interest and make reductions in principal. These are reflected in the following *coverage ratios:*

1. Interest Coverage Ratio $= \dfrac{\text{income before interest and income taxes}}{\text{interest charges}}$

2. Total Debt Coverage Ratio $=$
$$\dfrac{\text{income before interest and income taxes}}{\text{interest + principal charges}\left(\dfrac{1}{(1 - \text{combined federal and state tax rates})}\right)}$$

Realistically, lenders do not like to make loans to going businesses where the source of repayment is going to be the sale of a productive asset. In most cases, this means that the business plans to shrink in size at some point in the future. The sale of productive assets ordinarily is a "last-ditch maneuver" done by a company in trouble and scrambling for cash. Thus, we recommend that you not consider this as a viable source of loan repayment money.

The same conclusion holds with respect to "other borrowing" as a source of cash to repay loans. Can you imagine what might run through the mind of the loan officer if you told him, "I plan to repay this loan with money borrowed from another lender?" First, with this statement you are conceding that the project will not generate the means of repayment. In other words, it is a loser, and your NPV calculations are a fabrication. Second, you are branding yourself as a "roller," that is, a person who rolls loans from one lender to another as they come due. Every lender has some of these in his portfolio and probably wishes every day that he did not. Borrowing from another source to make debt repayments is an emergency measure and should not be considered as a viable source of funds to repay a loan.

The typical small business does not prepare *pro forma* statements, but the typical large business does. Seldom does a small business have to submit *pro forma* statements to obtain a loan. However, if it voluntarily did so, it surely would impress the loan officer with management's ability and competence in financial planning. Your accountant can prepare these statements very readily. You can do it without much trouble. The first step is to forecast sales for the next one to three years. Then, using past ratios of the various expenses to sales, estimate future expenses in relation to future sales. Of course, if you have knowledge of various expense items that may increase or decrease in relative terms, reflect these adjustments in your estimates. Subtract expenses from your gross profit (sales minus cost of goods sold) to determine earnings before taxes. Then estimate taxes and add the net profit totals each year to retained earnings.

To make up a *pro forma* statement of condition, first estimate the amount of cash, inventory, receivables, and fixed assets that will be needed to support and produce your forecasted sales total.

Then from future asset levels, subtract expected future levels of *existing* liabilities, capital, and new net profits to determine how much new money must be borrowed, if any, to finance the new asset levels.

Of course, if your purpose in seeking money is to finance a permanent increase in working capital, then *pro forma* statements are essential. As we have pointed out earlier in the book, one of the fundamental errors in business financial planning is to try to finance this permanent need for working capital with short-term loans. One of the chief benefits of preparing *pro forma* statements is that it forces a manager to think through the financial side of his business. He has to put down future sales, costs, assets, liabilities, and capital. These numbers become goals to work toward. If he is successful, salaries, profits, and owners' equity will grow to reward him.

Income Statements

Every incorporated business has to file an income statement with its annual tax return. Even if the business is an unincorporated sole proprietorship, then a Schedule C (Business Income) must be submitted with the owner's return. Whatever the case, the lender will want the most recent income statement and probably the last three. An income statement is an annual report card on management. It tells the lender something about the firm's ability to sell its product and control its costs. Hence, it reflects management's overall efficiency in running the enterprise. Again, we recommend having your accountant prepare this statement, but a cleanly typed statement prepared by you or your bookkeeper is better than no statement. As an alternative, you could photocopy the one submitted to the IRS.

At this point, another word of caution may be helpful to anyone contemplating "doctoring" a firm's statements of condition or income statements. It is against the law to submit a false financial statement to a lender as an inducement to make a loan. Resist the temptation.

Pro Forma Statements

A current statement of condition shows a firm's financial shape right now; it reflects everything that has happened to the business up to this point. It does not show how the firm's assets, liabilities, and capital will change after the loan proceeds are injected into the business. This question creates the need for projected or *pro forma* statements of condition and income statements. Both you and the lender would like to know how the business is going to fare financially with the new money. Remember, loans are repaid primarily with funds generated in the future, not the past.

INFORMATION THAT YOU MUST OR SHOULD PROVIDE THE LENDER

In this section, we will outline information that you should provide the lender. It will save time if you take this material with you to the initial interview.

Business History

Prepare a one page, typed summary of the firm's history. Indicate when and where the business was started and who the principals were and are. Comment on the business' overall success, when major new product lines were acquired or begun, and when major plant expansion or remodeling was accomplished. Lenders listen to all kinds of loan propositions in many industries, so the purpose of this brief history is to bring the loan officer "up to speed" quickly on your unique situation.

Statements of Condition

You must provide the lender with a current statement of condition on the business. The lender may request statements over the last three years. A statement of condition or balance sheet gives the lender a snapshot of the firm's assets, liabilities, and capital at one moment in time. Analysis of assets reveals how the firm has employed its "things owned" or resources. Analysis of liabilities reveals the nature and composition of "the claims of others" on the firm's resources. Analysis of capital reveals the absolute and relative size of "owners' claims on its resources." To a potential lender, capital indicates the extent to which the firm's assets could shrink without jeopardizing the security of the nonowner claim-holders.

Here are some tips on preparation of these statements. The best of all worlds is to have your accountant prepare audited financial statements. The next best situation is to have your accountant prepare unaudited statements. If you are unwilling to go this far, then prepare typed statements yourself. Do not scribble out a statement or try to pass off one that is a year old. The lender's immediate reaction to both of these acts is to reason that if the borrower does not care enough to prepare accurate and up-to-date statements on his own business, then why should he care enough to ensure timely repayment of someone else's money? To paraphrase Benjamin Franklin: "Sloppy in one thing; sloppy in everything."

Personal Financial Statements

In a closely held business, the owners almost always have to sign the notes in order to borrow. The lender knows that the financial fortunes of the business and the owners are one and the same. Hence, in virtually every case, the business owners must submit personal financial statements. It is a good practice to construct a personal financial statement every quarter anyway just to see where you stand, so it should be no problem making a copy of your statement and that of any other owners and have these ready to submit at the initial interview. In fact, you might stop by the lender's office ahead of time and obtain several blank financial statement forms.

List of Collateral

Unless your business qualifies for prime rate treatment, then expect to collateralize your loan. Typical collateral for a small business loan include land, buildings, equipment, vehicles, inventory, and receivables. Sometimes business loans are secured by cash value of life insurance, stocks, and real estate held by the owners. Therefore, it is a good idea to think ahead of the interview about what collateral you might offer if the lender requests it. This way, you will not make a mistake and offer as collateral something you have plans to sell shortly. Thus, have a typed list of the collateral that you propose to offer, its identification or serial number, and its estimated market value. More than likely, the value of the collateral must exceed the amount of the loan.

List of References

The lender must evaluate: (1) a firm's ability to pay and (2) its willingness to pay. Ability to pay depends on the business having the cash available when the loan payments are due. Willingness to pay involves management's decision to actually return money to a lender. A firm can have the ability to pay yet its management might lack the willingness to pay. Lenders measure management's willingness to pay primarily by its past willingness to pay. This is why lenders request a list of references from a potential borrower. These references can be other institutional lenders such as banks or finance companies, or they may be important trade credit sources such as suppliers. At any rate, prepare a list of references and take it to the initial interview.

PREPARATION FOR THE LOAN INTERVIEW

Now that we have outlined all the information that you should provide the lender, let's spend a few minutes thinking about your preparation for this interview.

Getting the Documents Together

The first step in preparation for the loan interview is to assemble all the necessary papers and documents to take to the interview.

Checklist for Documents to Take to the Loan Interview:

1. Business history
2. Statements of condition (three years)
3. Income statements (three years)
4. *Pro forma* statements of condition and income statement (one to three years)
5. Cash budget
6. NPV calculations (if long-term loan request)
7. Personal statements of condition (three years)
8. List of collateral (serial numbers and estimated market values)
9. List of references
10. Brochures and specifications on any equipment that you wish to finance

It may take several weeks to get all of these documents prepared and typed. In the loan interview, organization and neatness in your presentation will reflect professionalism on your part.

People To Take With You

Depending on the nature of the loan request, there are three or four people whom you may want to accompany you to the loan interview.

Accountant

Some managers who are primarily production- or sales-oriented feel uncomfortable trying to explain financial data to a professional loan officer. In such a case, it may be a good idea to invite your accountant to go with you and explain the loan request. If he prepared the statements, then he will be even more familiar with them. The value of a good accountant is far more than the fees that you will pay. The accuracy and preciseness that an accountant can lend to your financial statements enhances their credibility and improves your chances of getting the money you need.

Attorney

Attorneys often serve as financial counselors to small businesses. Sometimes managers like to take their attorney/counselor with them to explain the business' plans and needs for funds. They often can help you understand the legal ramifications of borrowing money and your rights as a borrower in the loan contract.

Small Business Consultants

As with everything else, among small business consultants there are good ones and bad ones. The good ones really can help you by providing an objective evaluation of every facet of your business. They may have knowledge of lenders who may be interested in financing your needs. If you have been working with a reliable consultant, you may consider taking him to the loan interview.

On the other hand, there are "rip-off artists" posing as small business consultants. Their aims are many. Some may want to evaluate your business with an eye toward buying it. They may come up with a phony list of problems that you are supposed to have and then offer you 50¢ on the dollar to relieve you of the burdens. Others may be trying to line you up with unscrupulous lenders who want a high rate for funds. In this situation, the so-called consultant is trying to earn a fee from you for finding the funds and from the source of money for finding the sucker. Beware! Check the qualifications of these consultants with your banker or local chamber of commerce.

College Business Consultants

In recent years, a number of college business departments have developed "small business development centers." Their primary function is to assist small and growing businesses. These centers may have professors and graduate students available to do feasibility studies, provide an objective evaluation of your business, and provide counseling to assist you in solving all kinds of problems.

Make an Appointment

Loan officers are busy people and so are you. The professional way to apply for a loan is to call the loan officer several days ahead of time and arrange an appointment that is mutually convenient.

Prepare Answers to the Three
Anticipated Questions

Earlier in this chapter, we posed the three key questions that every lender asks:

1. What is the purpose of the loan?
2. How much money do you need?
3. What are the sources of repayment?

We suggest that you think through your responses to these questions so that you can provide the lender with a clear, concise answer to each question. Of course, you have your financial statements that reveal the purpose, need, and source of repayment, so you should have no trouble formulating answers.

SUMMARY

Here are the key points in this chapter:

1. Start your search for the money you need at a bank. If the banker cannot help you, usually he can recommend a lender who can.

2. Every lender asks a potential borrower three questions:

    (a)   What is the purpose of the loan?
    (b)   How much money do you need?
    (c)   What are the sources of repayment?

    Be ready to answer these questions.

3. Below is a checklist of the documents that you should take to the loan interview:

   (a) Business history
   (b) Statements of condition (three years)
   (c) Income statement (three years)
   (d) *Pro forma* statements of condition and income statements (one to three years)
   (e) Cash budget
   (f) NPV calculations (long-term loan request)
   (g) Personal statements of condition (three years)
   (h) List of collateral (serial numbers and estimated market values)
   (i) List of references
   (j) Brochures and specifications on any equipment that you wish to finance

4. The care with which you assemble the information in item 3 has a bearing on whether you can borrow the money you need.

6

What the Lender Will Do With Your Application

In Chapter 5, we discussed "How to Apply for the Money You Need." Your "application" for a loan consists primarily of all the documents and information that you provided the lender at the initial interview. The process of investigation and evaluation of this package of material and information is called *credit analysis.*

With large lenders, the loan officer will have the responsibility to obtain from you the necessary statements and most of the information required in the loan application. The application then is forwarded to a credit department for analysis and recommendation. When this process is completed, it is the responsibility of the loan officer or loan committee (in the case of large loans) to make the final decision whether or not to approve the loan. This process may take anywhere from three days to a month.

In this chapter, we shall: (1) explore the nature and sources of the risks faced by business borrowers and their creditors, (2) note the relationship between the credit risk and credit analysis, (3) analyze in depth the *5 Cs* of credit analysis, and (4) learn the sources of credit information to the lender.

SOURCES AND TYPES OF BUSINESS RISKS

When a loan is made to a firm, the lender, in effect, becomes a "partner" with the company and, as such, is exposed to all the risks to which the business is exposed. You hear the term "risk" bandied about in every discussion involving lending. In this context, risk means the possibility of loss. Credit analysis involves, in large part, the identification and evaluation of the sources and types of risks that borrowers and lenders face. We believe that if you understand better the external sources and types of business risks, you can improve your handling of these risks and therefore present a creditworthy application to potential lenders.

External Sources of Business Risks

By "external" sources of business risks, we mean those sources outside of the firm and largely outside the control of management.

Social

A firm may suffer losses and have to default or delay payment of loans because of the actions of people who adversely affect it. Theft, vandalism, arson, riot, strikes, and accidents are the principal business risks of a social origin.

Physical

A firm also may sustain losses from sources that have a physical origin. These sources of risk include fire, floods, drought, tornadoes, hurricanes, lightning, rain, hail, landslides, and earthquakes.

Economic

Businesses are exposed to risks caused by fluctuations in economic activity. The ability of most firms to repay loans is lessened in one way or another when the economy suffers a recession or depression and income and employment decline. Also, many firms are adversely affected during periods of inflation. Those businesses that are unable to raise prices in the face of cost increases are prime candidates to default on loans.

Types of Business Risks — SIDE

1. Personal Risks

A firm may suffer a serious loss through the premature death or disability of a key employee. Sales or production may decline, and the business may be unable to meet its loan obligations. In addition, a business is exposed to personal risks when it accepts that part of the death or disability risk of its employees transferred to it under workmen's compensation laws or by employment contracts.

2. Property Risks   many

Businesses lose billions of dollars' worth of property annually. The sources of these losses are social, physical, and economic. The loss of property may impair a firm's ability to repay its loans.

3. Liability Risks

Like people, firms are liable to others for bodily injury or property damage. This liability could arise from the activities of employees and agents as well as the products and services sold by the firm. Obviously, a large award under a liability suit could undermine a company's ability to pay its debts.

THE CREDIT RISK AND CREDIT ANALYSIS   HEADLINE

Nature and Sources of the Credit Risk — SIDE

The possibility of loss to a lender through default is called the *credit risk*. When a lender extends credit, it gives the borrower money to use now in return for the promise to repay money in the future. The lender, of course, expects repayment on schedule unless the borrower is either (1) unable or (2) unwilling to discharge the obligation. These two factors are the sources of the credit risk.

Nature and Objectives of Business Credit Analysis — SIDE

The purpose of business credit analysis is to evaluate the sources of the credit risk that the lender assumes—the firm's ability and willingness to repay a loan in the future. The determination of a firm's future ability to repay a loan requires an evaluation of the possible risks to which it might be exposed, and an analysis of the company's past and *pro forma* statements of condition and income. An evaluation of a company's future willingness to pay its debts involves primarily an investigation of its past willingness to pay. It also entails the investigation of the personal financial condition and business dealings of the firm's principal officers. The basic presumption is that people who have demonstrated a willingness to meet their obligations in the past and who have a history of honesty in dealings will continue to exhibit these characteristics in the future. Of course, there are surprises, but the basic tendency is true.

Thus, at this point, it should be clear why the lender will request so much information about your business and you. All of this information enables the lender to evaluate the two sources of the credit risk to which it will be exposed—a firm's ability and willingness to repay the proposed loan.

The Lender's Method's of Handling the Credit Risk ~ SIDE

Every loan involves a credit risk. Think of all the bad things that could happen to GM, Exxon, or AT&T that could impair the ability of any one of these firm's ability to pay. Once upon a time, who thought Chrysler ever would have financial problems? After a credit analyst has evaluated the sources and magnitude of a firm's credit risk the next step is for the loan officer to determine the best approach to handle the loan request. The area of risk management offers three methods of dealing with risk that lenders may apply to management of the credit risk. These are: (1) avoidance, (2) loss prevention and control, and (3) transfer.

(for interest)

Avoidance
The first alternative open to a lender is to avoid the credit risk and decline the loan request. This would occur if, given the interest rate and other fees that may be charged, the chance of loss on the loan is too great to justify assumption of the risk, even after the lender and borrower have used every technique to eliminate, con-

trol, or transfer the risk. In other words, sometimes from a lender's perspective, it is best just to shake hands and walk away from the deal.

2. **Loss Prevention and Control**

If a lender decides to assume the credit risk (and every loan involves a chance of loss), it may be only upon the condition that the firm agrees to certain provisions designed to prevent and control possible loss to the lender. For example, a lender might specify that your business maintain a minimum ratio of current assets, restrict officers' salaries, and limit additional borrowing. These provisions are designed to enhance your firm's ability to repay the loan on schedule. A periodic visit by the loan officer to the borrower's place of business also is an important loss prevention and control technique.

3. **Loss Transfer**

Closely associated with loss prevention and control is the technique of loss transfer, which involves a lender shifting all or part of the credit risk to a third party or to the borrower. For example, the requirement that you have a cosigner, purchase credit life insurance, maintain adequate property and casualty insurance, or pledge collateral such as land, equipment, or stock result in a transfer of all or part of the credit risk from the lender.

THE 5 Cs OF CREDIT ANALYSIS

How will the lender reach the decision that your business has the ability and willingness to pay? The time-honored way involves an analysis of the 5 Cs of credit: (1) character, (2) capacity, (3) capital, (4) conditions, and (5) collateral. Everything that bears upon your firm's ability and willingness to pay can be analyzed within the framework of the famous 5 Cs. Your understanding of them will help you provide better documents and information to enhance your chances of passing the 5 Cs test and receiving the money you need.

Character

Meaning

Virtually every lender will tell you that character of the borrower is the most important consideration in their decision to make a loan. By character we mean the entire set of qualities having to do with how a person conducts his business and personal affairs. Character covers such things as how you deal with the public. Does your firm produce a quality product or service and attempt to sell it at a fair price? Does it provide service to customers after a sale? Character covers how you deal with your employees. Indeed, character includes your past determination and record with respect to paying suppliers and other lenders on time. A reflection of your character is your advertising. Does your firm engage in misleading advertising? Another important facet of character is your "stick-to-it-ive-ness," that is, how you perform when the going gets tough. We all know people who when faced with adversity and hardship just collapse and quit. The thousands of people who walk away from charge card debts every year are good examples of quitters. Experienced lenders know that if the going does get tough in a business, the borrower with character somehow will find a way to pay the loan.

Measurement and Evaluation

At first thought, you might think that there are no quantitative measures of character. But there are a few. Here is a partial list of quantitative indications of positive character are

- zero judgments against your firm, you, or other owners
- zero defaults or "slow pays" on your credit record
- zero complaints against your firm at the Better Business Bureau
- zero overdrafts at the bank, now or in the past

Of course, there are many aspects of character evaluation that are subjective. For example, a neat, clean, orderly looking place of business is indicative of caring management and shows respect for employees and customers. On the other hand, an attitude of carelessness and lack of concern suggests character defects. Of course, each of these examples is difficult to judge, but they can be judged.

The "bottom line" on character measurement and evaluation is that a person either is honest or he is not. How can a borrower be "mostly honest" or of "partial good character"? If a borrower wants to beat a lender out of money, he can do it. He will think how to do it 24 hours a day, while the lender has a portfolio of borrowers to worry about. A lender cannot charge a high enough interest rate to cover a default. Moreover, he will have additional expenses chasing a wayward borrower.

We want to emphasize that the ability to borrow hinges strongly on character. Legitimate lenders ordinarily decline loan requests from borrowers who are not of good character. Therefore, a clean business and personal record will pay handsomely when your loan request is analyzed.

Capacity - SIDE

Meaning

As with character, capacity has several dimensions. First, capacity can refer to the physical capacity of your manufacturing facilities or sales outlets. What is your firm's capacity to produce or sell enough products to pay the loan? Second, capacity can refer to managerial capacity. The question here is do you and your employees have the knowledge and ability to expand sales and control costs in good and bad times. Finally, capacity can refer to (also) your firm's ability to generate enough cash over the cash cycle to pay short-term loans and over the long-run to pay long-term loans.

Measurement and Evaluation

Physical capacity for a manufacturing firm is determined by the size of the plant, number of machines, employment, number of shifts in a work week, and ready availability of raw materials. The question with respect to physical capacity is whether the present or prospective productive resources are sufficient to meet sales objectives. Every production manager has data on production by period, so it can be provided quite easily to the lender.

With respect to a retail and wholesale operation, physical capacity depends on the space available, type of merchandise, number of employees, competition, and many other factors. Analysis of the trend in sales data for each outlet and a comparison of the totals with those of competitors generally will provide the lender with insight into physical capacity.

With respect to managerial capacity, a good measure of this is the bottom line on your income statement. Good profits usually indicate good management, that management knows how to increase sales and/or control costs, and that management knows how to survive in tough times of rapid inflation and high interest rates. However, a firm can have good profits, yet be cash short on its statement of condition or possibly have outmoded or worn out plant and equipment. Therefore, good liquidity and quality facilities and equipment reflect managerial capacity. The idea here is that "if management messes up the 'little things,' they will mess up the 'big things.' " Attention to detail is reflected in the accuracy and appearance of the document submitted at the loan interview and the appearance and condition of the place of business.

Last, a firm's *debt payment capacity* depends on every facet of the business. In a nutshell, it includes the firm's ability to sell products and services, collect in a timely manner the receivables generated, manage the cash assets of the business, and earn net profits. If a business can do these things well, it usually has good debt payment capacity.

Capital - SIDE

Meaning
Capital includes those accounts on the right-hand side of the statement of condition that show how many dollars the owners of

the business have contributed toward financing of the firm's assets.

Measurement and Evaluation

Capital usually includes the common stock and retained earnings accounts. *Liabilities* are the accounts on the right-hand side of the statement of condition that show how many dollars lenders, suppliers and others have contributed toward financing the firm's assets. From a lender's standpoint, capital's primary function is to protect the lender's capital from possible loss. An example should clarify this very important point. Suppose that a business shows a net loss on its income statement. This means that the firm's expenses have exceeded its income and it has paid out more cash than it received. This loss is shown on the statement of condition by a decrease in capital (owners' claim on assets) and a decrease in cash on the left-hand side. Remember a balance sheet must balance. If there are less assets available, then the owners' claim on the right-hand side must shrink. It is a fact of life that liability holders are not going to step forward and say "reduce my claim on your assets so your balance sheet will balance."

Now to the main point. How much capital a firm has measures how much assets can decline without jeopardizing liability holders such as lenders. The more capital a firm has, the larger the losses a firm can absorb from any source (theft, arson, natural disaster, operating losses, or whatever) without causing the claims of liability holder to exceed available assets.

Thus, it should be clear that a potential lender would want to analyze a firm's absolute and relative amount of capital. It does so, in part, through evaluation of the following *capital ratios:*

1. Debt-to-Equity Ratio $= \dfrac{\text{total liablities}}{\text{owners' equity}}$

2. Debt-to-Assets Ratio $= \dfrac{\text{total liabilities}}{\text{total assets}}$

The first ratio measures the extent to which the claims of the liability holders exceeds the claim of owners. Both ratios also measure *financial leverage,* the extent to which the firm has used borrowed funds to finance assets. The higher these ratios, the greater the risk that a potential lender takes if it commits funds to the firm.

This discussion of capital also brings to the surface the age-old struggle between the creditors and a firm's owners. Owners would like to have a minimum amount of capital because it raises the return on equity capital and because they may have other uses for the funds such as investment in other businesses. On the other hand, as we have mentioned, lenders want owners to have a large capital base in order to have more protection from potential losses. This confrontation over capital is sometimes called the *capital dilemma.*

You must appreciate this dilemma from the lender's viewpoint. Why should he commit more funds to the business than you do? Why should he assume more of the risk of failure for a limited reward, while the owners risk less and stand to receive a large reward if the business is a success? Now you should understand why capital is an important one of the 5 Cs of credit.

Conditions

Meaning
The term "conditions" in a credit analysis context refers to at least four factors bearing upon a lenders decision to extend credit. These include: (1) the financial condition of the company, (2) the condition of the lender, (3) the condition of the company and credit markets and (4) the conditions of the specific markets in which the firm operates.

Measurement and Evaluation
The financial condition of the company means essentially the condition of the firm's assets, liquidity, capital adequacy, and profitability. Information on the condition of a firm's assets can be obtained from management, an outside appraisal, and an inspection visit by the lender. Information about a firm's liquidity, capital adequacy, and profitability, both past and prospective, is

obtained primarily through analysis of the company's financial statements. Of course, a large part of credit analysis centers on the condition of the prospective borrower.

It may or may not surprise you that the condition of the lender may have a bearing on the credit decision. In recent periods of tight money, many lenders simply did not have the funds to lend. That is, the liquidity position of the lenders did not permit further reduction in cash levels. In such situations, a number of worthwhile borrowers must be told to seek funds elsewhere or postpone their loan request until credit conditions ease.

In addition to credit conditions, the condition of the economy in general affects lenders' ability and willingness to lend. For example, when the economy enters a recession, a lender reasons that rising unemployment and falling income will reduce a prospective borrower's sales, profits, cash flow, and hence, debt paying ability. In other words, the overall risk level in the economy rises and affects negatively virtually every borrower's ability and, perhaps, willingness to pay.

Inflation also impacts negatively on the credit decision. Inflation leads to higher interest rates which means that borrowers have to earn more income to pay the interest. During inflationary periods, some firms are able to raise their prices more easily than others. Moreover, the increase in operating cost hits some businesses harder than others. The sum and substance is that inflation increases the possibility that some firms may not be able to repay their loans on schedule. Hence, both recession and inflation make lenders more cautious about the commitment of funds.

Collateral

Meaning
Collateral refers to any type of security that a borrower offers the lender as a secondary source of repayment. Collateral may include any kind of property, but it also covers the use of guarantors or cosigners. The primary sources of repayment, of course, are the conversion of receivables into cash and profits. Secondary sources of repayment are those that must be used if the primary ones fail. Calling on a secondary source of repayment would involve

conversion of collateral into cash or requesting a guarantor or co-signer to step up and repay a loan.

Measurement and Evaluation

From a risk management point of view, the primary function of collateral is to transfer part of the credit risk to the borrower or a third party. Therefore, the amount of risk that is transferred depends on the quantity and quality of the collateral. Some collateral such as savings accounts, CDs, and U.S. Treasury bonds have a more stable value than inventory, receivables, and over-the-counter stocks. Some collateral, such as savings accounts and CDs, is more liquid (that is, able to be converted into cash quickly and at little or no discount) than leasehold improvements and ladies dresses that may sell for 25 cents on the dollar. Therefore, lenders evaluate closely the quantity and quality of collateral relative to the amount of a proposed loan. Generally, if collateral is requested by a lender, he wants a collateral value greater than the amount of the loan. In other words, you can only borrow a fraction of the value of the collateral. For example, typical loan advances will be limited to 80 percent on trucks, appliances, and other durable goods, 50 percent on consumables such as clothing, 80 percent on land and buildings, and 50 percent on over-the-counter stocks.

A fundamental credit principle is that "collateral does not make the loan." This means that if a lender has to look to secondary sources of repayment, he probably will suffer a loss on the loan and incur costs of collection. However, collateral is like an insurance policy that provides cash if a loss occurs. Now that you know the purpose of collateral, you should not be affronted if the lender requests collateral.

SOURCES OF CREDIT INFORMATION

At large banks, commercial finance companies, and leasing companies, it is the credit department that evaluates the 5Cs for a loan application. At some institutions, the contact loan officer performs this function. Credit departments are staffed with people experienced in financial analysis. That is, they know how to evaluate financial statements of all kinds and a firm's ability and willingness to pay. To perform this financial analysis, the credit department assembles and compiles information about: (1) the firm itself and (2) the industry in which it operates.

For the Firm

The Firm's Officers

As we discussed in the last chapter, a firm's officers or owners usually are the primary source of financial and other information on the company. The bulk of this information is received at the initial interview by the loan officer who turns it over to the credit department and discusses the proposed credit extension.

Credit Files

Large lenders maintain credit files on present and prospective business borrowers in their market area. These files contain financial statements, a record of any past borrowing, articles from newspapers and trade journals, and other bits of data about the firm. Even if a firm is not presently a customer of the lender, if the company is important in its market area, an aggressive credit department manager will have a file established.

Financial Statements

Statements of condition and income statements represent hard evidence on a company's past ability to pay and, as such, are vital sources of information. In addition, a cash budget, *pro forma* statements of condition and income, and a capital budget supported by NPV calculations provide information about a firm's expected ability to pay. When the credit department receives these statements, the data are arranged on "spread sheets," by years, to facilitate analysis.

Credit Bureaus

An important source of credit information on individuals and, to a lesser extent, on local businesses is the credit bureau. Credit bureaus provide written and telephone reports on the creditworthiness of individuals and firms. In addition, these bureaus issue weekly or bimonthly reports containing information about bankruptcies filed, recordings of real estate mortgages, judgements granted, and other significant happenings that might reflect on the ability and willingness of local citizens and businesses to pay their financial obligations.

Dun and Bradstreet, Inc.

Most lenders rely extensively on Dun and Bradstreet, Inc. (D&B) for credit information on prospective borrowers. The famous D&B rating on a firm provides, with the aid of a key, the estimated net worth and a credit appraisal (high, good, fair, or limited) for companies on which D&B has adequate information. Besides the rating services, D&B will issue written credit reports that contain a brief history of a company and its principal officers, the nature of the business, certain financial information, and the results of a check with the firm's suppliers as to their experience with the company.

Other Lenders

Lenders share credit information with each other. For example, from another lender a credit analyst can learn very quickly the borrowing record, and sometimes other information, about financial strengths and weaknesses of a prospective borrower.

The Firm's Suppliers and Customers

When feasible, a credit analyst will contact several of the prospective business borrower's suppliers and customers. The firm's suppliers can indicate their payment experience with the company. The firm's customers can provide valuable information on the quality of the company's services or products and insight into the honesty and integrity of the company's management.

Public Records

Public records are a vital source of credit information. Courthouse records show recorded mortgages, recorded lease assignments, bankruptcy or default judgement filings, and tax liens. In most states, the Secretary of State's Office contains recordings of security interest under the Uniform Commercial Code.

For the Industry

The next task for a credit analyst is to compare operating and financial data for the firm under consideration with similar data for other firms in the industry and with industry averages. In addition, a credit analyst must become familiar with new developments and trends in the industry to appraise the ability of the firm to compete in the future. The primary sources of information at the industry level are described below.

Robert Morris Associates *Annual Statement Studies*

One of the most widely used sources of industry data is the Robert Morris Associates *Annual Statement Studies*. (Robert Morris Associates is the national association of bank loan and credit officers). The publication shows, for almost 300 lines of business and for several classes of firm size, the average ratios for major asset, liability, income, and expense items. In addition, a number of average operating ratios are presented. These industry ratios enable a credit analyst to determine if your firm is above average, average, or below average with respect to liquidity, capital adequacy, use of debt, profitability and other financial aspects of business.

Moody's and Standard and Poor's

Besides providing up-to-date financial information on large, individual firms, Moody's Investors Service and Standard and Poor's Corporation provide excellent sources of industry data. In addition, the periodic analysis provided by industry specialists at these companies is especially valuable.

Trade Publications and Journals

In order to search developments in a particular industry, a credit analyst must rely considerably on trade publications and journals. The libraries at large banks and commercial finance companies subscribe to most of this literature. Therefore, it is a good idea to make sure that your firm takes subscriptions to these publications so that a lender will not be more current than you are in your own field.

Government Publications

Over the last thirty years, the volume of government publications has mushroomed. Credit analysts have discovered the wealth of information about American and foreign industry and trade contained in these documents.

SUMMARY

Here are the key points in this chapter:

1. When a lender commits funds to your business, he becomes a partner and shares in the fortunes of that company. He is exposed to all the risks surrounding the firm.

2. Credit analysts seek to evaluate the sources of the credit risk, that is, the firm's ability and willingness to repay a loan in the future.

3. Lenders have three methods of dealing with the credit risk:

    (a) Avoidance
    (b) Loss prevention and control
    (c) Transfer

4. The 5 Cs of credit analysis are:

    (a) Character
    (b) Capacity
    (c) Capital
    (d) Conditions
    (e) Collateral

Character is the most important.

7
Closing the Loan
and Getting the Money

TITLE

For the inexperienced, a loan closing can be a traumatic event. There you are, signing papers with fine print that you hesitate to read because you do not want to appear dumb. You just know that you are signing your life away. Visions of a stay in the "poor house" dance through your head. You probably experienced all of these feelings when you closed your first home loan. Total unpleasantness!

The goal in this chapter is to walk you through all the steps and documents involved in closing a commercial loan. We want you to enjoy the occasion. After all, you are getting the money you need and, hopefully, business expansion and profits are just around the corner. The major topics covered in this chapter are: (1) loan approvals, (2) loan commitments, (3) loan documentation, (4) the closing itself, and (5) disbursement of funds. This chapter is not intended in any way to give any type of legal advice. It will outline procedures and head you in the right direction to get the professional help you might need.

LOAN APPROVAL *HEADLINE*

After the lender has completed his credit analysis, he has three options:

92

1. Approve your loan as you requested it
2. Disapprove your loan
3. Agree to make the loan provided certain additional conditions can be met

If the loan is approved as requested then you have no problem. The wheels are set in motion.

If your loan is disapproved, then obviously you have a problem. However, in business lending the disapproval process usually is not cut and dried. If the lender took the time to listen to your story, take your application, and analyze the application in detail and at considerable expense, then he may have made a preliminary conditional decision about your loan. First, if the loan request had not met the lender's loan policy specifications, he would have told you early and the application would not have gone further. Every lender has a written loan policy that represents guidelines for the types of loans that the lender wishes to make as well as guidelines for maturities, interest rates, fees, and security requirements. For example, if you have requested a loan to open an office far outside the lender's market area, the lender probably would have denied the request at the loan interview. If your initial request had run counter to the lender's loan policy, then at that point he might have offered suggestions on another source of funds or suggested certain conditions that you would need to meet before he would accept an application. Such conditions could include a requirement that you put additional capital in the business or provide more information on the project to be financed.

Alternative #3 above is encountered often and may be the most typical case. After analysis of your request, the lender may approve the loan, provided that you meet certain conditions such as pledging additional collateral, obtaining outside guarantors, agreeing to shorter repayment terms, etc. Typically, he will call you and explain these additional conditions. Do not be afraid to negotiate with the lender. However, if his requirements are valid, practical, and reasonable, then go along with them.

LOAN COMMITMENTS

After the loan has been approved and all the terms and conditions have been agreed to by both you and the lender, then the lender will make a commitment to you. Commitments take two forms: (1) oral and (2) written.

Oral Commitments

Oral commitments usually are made on small loans that will be made immediately. The lender will call and say "Fred, your truck loan is approved." The note and necessary documents are signed and a check is drawn to the business and the vendor and that is about it.

Written Commitments

If the loan is more complicated and involves a lot of money, then the lender will write you a commitment letter. If a letter is not offered, for your protection ask the lender for one. The commitment letter will be addressed to the business or its officers and will state what the lender commits to do, provided that the borrower meets certain terms and conditions. A typical commitment letter will:

1. Identify the parties (borrower and lender).
2. State the form of the loan, the amount of the loan, repayment terms, and interest rate.
3. State any commitment fees required.
4. Outline collateral to be taken, agreements to be entered into, guarantees required, and other documents necessary to close the loan.
5. Specify the expiration date for the commitment.
6. State that legal fees, if any, will be borne by the borrower.
7. Have a designated place for you to sign to indicate your acceptance of the commitment.

Before you accept the commitment, read the letter carefully to make certain that you are satisfied with it and understand what needs to be done to close the loan. At this point, it is a good idea to consult with your attorney to make sure everything is in order. It is a good idea to have your attorney go with you at the loan closing to check documentation from your point of view. The lender will have counsel representing him to make certain that all documents are properly drawn and executed before he advances any funds.

You as borrower normally are required to pay legal expenses incurred by the lender as well as any you will incur. If the lender uses his in-house counsel, usually there is no charge. The requirement that you pay legal fees normally will be spelled out in the commitment letter. If there is any confusion on this point, resolve it quickly so that there are no misunderstandings or holdups at the closing.

Commitment Fees

One point of clarification is in order here. In Chapter 2, we told you that a bank ordinarily will inform you by letter if it grants you a line of credit. However, such letters are normally informal and can be canceled virtually at the bank's option. The written commitments that we are discussing in this section are legally binding as long as their terms and conditions are met.

For your commitment, be prepared to pay a commitment fee— especially in connection with complicated loans or loans to be closed or disbursed at a relatively distant future time such as three to six months from the commitment date. You might look upon this fee as a reservation fee for the money you need. From the lender's point of view, the fee is justified because the lender must find funding to accommodate your request.

DOCUMENTATION

Loan documents are legal instruments that obligate borrowers to repay loans, effect pledges of collateral, and reduce to writing what the borrower and lender agree to do as long as the loan is outstanding. This section of the chapter is long and some of you may think it is boring. But, believe us, it is important in the lending process. Knowledge of the documentation requirements will raise your status in the eyes of everyone at the closing. However, "a little learning is a dangerous thing," so do not "sound off" at the closing like you are an expert. Just acknowledge quietly that you know what is going on.

Authority to Borrow

Every borrower must demonstrate to the lender his authority to borrow.

Individuals
If you are in business as a proprietor, you can obligate yourself and your business by signing your name. No other authorization is necessary.

Partnerships
Partnerships normally have partnership agreements executed by the partners. Such agreements may authorize one partner to obligate the partnership for loans. You will be required to submit a copy of the agreement to the lender. In the absence of such a specification in a partnership agreement, either all partners must sign documents or your attorney can draw a special authorization for borrowing.

Corporations.
For corporate borrowing, it is necessary to submit a written resolution of the corporation's board of directors that authorizes the borrowing and designates the corporate officers who may obligate the corporation. Most lenders have forms that may be used for this type of authority to borrow.

Obligations and Terms to Repay Borrowed Money

At the loan closing, you will be required to sign a document that obligates you or your company to repay the lender. Depending on the kind of loan, these documents may be notes or leases.

Notes

Notes are promises to pay that have a maker and a payee. You as borrower are the maker or promisor and the lender is the payee or promisee to whom you promise to repay the borrowed money in accordance with the terms and conditions of the notes. There are two types of notes: (1) form notes and (2) tailor-made notes.

Form Notes. Form notes are preprinted and used in routine loans such as equipment finance, vehicle finance, and short-term working capital loans. Language in these notes is pretty much standard, but will vary from state-to-state to reflect differences in laws.

Tailor-Made Notes. Tailor-made notes usually are drawn by the lender's attorney to fit an individual transaction where a form note would not work. In large complicated loans, tailor-made notes usually are the rule.

Note Terms. In lending there is a certain jargon that borrowers should understand concerning repayment terms and note types.

Time notes are notes used for specific one-time loan transactions. The term "time note" arose because the obligation is to be repaid at some specific date or point in time. Time notes normally are used when the loan is to be repaid in less than one year. Time notes usually are made for periods of 30, 60, 90, or 180 days.

Demand notes are obligations to pay money upon demand by the lender. Ordinarily demand notes are not used in business loans. Demand loans usually are made to borrowers who pledge highly liquid collateral such as stocks and bonds and who seek to make a business investment in other securities or make a direct capital commitment in a business. Demand loans may be called at any time and, if the borrowers cannot pay, any collateral pledged can be sold to retire the debt.

In some cases, demand notes are used for advances under short-term lines of credit to avoid renewals and extra paper work. For example, in Chapter 2 the NOEL Company's lender might ask NOEL's authorized officer to sign demand notes each time the company drew on its line of credit. If so, NOEL pays interest monthly on the daily outstanding balance of its obligations and makes principal payments as its cash flow is sufficient to do so. At any rate, NOEL repays all of its loans in one year.

Installment notes simply set the prearranged dates of installment payments due. Payments of interest and principal may be made monthly, quarterly, semiannually or annually. In general, almost any installment payment program can be agreed upon to fit the cash timing of the borrower. However, the terms listed above are typical.

Revolving notes are used with revolving credit agreements that allow a firm to borrow up to a certain maximum amount and repay as cash flow is generated but have the additional flexibility of allowing the borrower to obtain new funds as needed. Revolving credit agreements usually are made for a period of more than one year, but normally no longer than for three or four years. It is a flexible form of financing that is usually secured and used in special lending situations such as accounts receivable and inventory financing made by commercial finance companies specializing in these services.

Leases

Leases are contracts to make periodic payments for the use of assets. Leased assets range from everyday items such as delivery trucks and buildings to multimillion dollar aircraft and specialized and expensive equipment. Leasing could be the subject of another book so only the bare basics will be covered in this one. Leases can be divided into two broad categories: (1) true leases and (2) lease-purchase agreements.

A *true lease* is an arms'-length-transaction (both parties are independent of each other) in which the lessee rents an asset from the owner or lessor. Periodic lease payments are made for the specified period of the lease. When the last contracted payment is made, the lessee may have an option to buy the leased asset at fair market value. True leases can be complicated from an accounting and tax point of view. When entering into any lease, make sure that you know your legal obligation under the lease agreement.

Lease-purchase contracts are structured like leases, but the lessee agrees to buy the leased asset at the end of the lease in accordance with an agreed or stipulated price. Here again make sure that you know your legal, accounting, and tax obligations under any lease purchase contracts that you sign. Similar to lease-purchase contracts are *conditional sales contracts* which are contracts for the sale of an asset by a seller where title is retained by the seller until all payments are made. Hence, your purchase of the asset is conditioned on your making the specified payments. Heavy equipment often is sold in this manner.

Pledges of Collateral

First, in case the primary source of cash does not materialize, lenders require collateral as a secondary source of repayment to secure their loans. The primary forms of collateral are (1) real estate, (2) chattles, (3) intangibles owned, (4) borrowed assets pledges through hypothecation, and (5) cosigners or guarantors.

Real Estate

To pledge real estate as collateral, the lender requires (depending on the state) a mortgage or deed of trust in the real estate. These documents are prepared by attorneys who, after a search of the public real estate records, certify to the lender that he has a valid claim on the property if the terms of the note are not met and foreclosure is necessary. Laws governing real estate vary from state-to-state so rely on your attorney to handle real estate transactions for you.

Most lenders require a title insurance policy to guarantee for them clear title to the property if some unknown factor arises that clouds title to real estate pledged. You will be expected to pay for this insurance. In addition, you should purchase title insurance for your own protection.

Chattles

Chattles include any asset not real estate or intangible. Equipment, vehicles, furniture, fixtures, inventory, and machinery are chattles.

To pledge chattles, you will be required to execute a security agreement that gives the lender a security interest in the pledged assets. The security agreement will describe the assets and their location. To perfect their security interest in the collateral, a legal filing of public notice will be made. Filing places other lenders on notice that your assets have been taken as collateral. Again, laws and procedures vary from state-to-state so rely on your attorney if there are any questions on pledging chattles. For simple transactions like purchasing and financing a small piece of equipment, standard forms can be used. For more complicated transactions, specially drawn documents may be needed.

Intangibles

An *intangible* is any type of collateral that is neither real estate nor chattle. Intangibles include stocks, bonds, partnership interests, patents, contract rights, accounts receivable, notes receivable, or any other claim on value.

Intangibles are assigned as collateral either by security agreement or by physical possession by the lender. For intangibles such as patents and partnership interests, a written assignment must be drawn and filings made in public records. For stocks and bonds, physical possession by the lender is sufficient. A simple pledge of stock requires a note, a stock power of attorney, and a Federal Reserve Regulation "U" disclosure form indicating the purpose of the loan. However, when other intangibles are involved, rely on legal counsel to prepare documents and explain the pledge to you.

Hypothecation

Hypothecation of collateral simply means that the owner of the asset agrees in writing to allow you to pledge his collateral to secure your loan. A typical case occurs when an individual pledges personal assets as security for a business loan. If this happens, to make such a pledge, you must execute a hypothecation agreement.

Cosigners, Guarantors, and Endorsers

For convenience of explanation we shall include cosigners, guarantors, and endorsers under the general heading of pledges of collateral. It is important that you learn that the legal obligation of each signer differs. A *cosigner* is a maker of the note and has an obligation to pay if any other maker fails to pay. Guarantors may be (1) limited or (2) unlimited. A *limited guarantor* is obligated to pay only a specific amount if the makers fail to pay. For example, a limited guarantor on a $100,000 loan may be obligated to pay only $10,000 if that is the amount spelled out in the guaranty agreement. On the other hand, an *unlimited guarantor* has to step up and make all missed payments until the note is fully paid or the makers begin to pay or pay the note in full depending on the agreement. An *endorser* pays only if the original makers cannot pay, but after the lender has exhausted all remedies to collect including sale of collateral.

Agreements

All documents used in lending money are agreements of one type or another. The note is an agreement to repay the borrowed money and collateral pledges are agreements to secure the loan. In addition to these agreements, lenders may require a formal written statement of the verbally agreed-to loan transaction. This document simply puts in words the agreed terms and conditions of the relationship between the borrower and the lender. This is called the loan agreement.

Loan Agreements

Loan agreements take a number of forms but basically they can be classified as (1) simple or (2) comprehensive.

A *simple agreement* can be the commitment letter itself if it spells out the responsibilities of the parties and is accepted in writing by the borrower. As stated earlier, review the commitment letter carefully and understand fully what is required of you as a borrower. If the letter calls for a separate, more comprehensive loan agreement, the commitment letter may spell out the most important requirements of that agreement, but it will clearly state that it is to be separate and not limited in scope to the few requirements cited in the letter.

A *comprehensive agreement* spells out mutual understandings between the borrower and lender and usually follows a more or less standard format. These agreements may be drawn by your attorney, but most often are drawn by the lender's counsel. Of course, your attorney should review it and advise you as necessary. Comprehensive agreements generally contain the following sections:

I.   A *statement of the transaction* naming borrower, lender, amounts, rates, maturity, and terms.

II. A *definition section* defining terms to be used in the agreement.

III. A *representations and warranties* section in which the borrower states such items as (1) that the financial statements are accurate, (2) that the borrowing is authorized, and (3) that all taxes have been paid. In general, the borrower assures the lender that his business is being run properly and the transaction is authorized.

IV. An *affirmative covenants section* in which the borrower promises to do certain things as long as the loan is outstanding. Covenants include promises: (1) to pay taxes on time, (2) to provide financial statements and other information to the lender, (3) to maintain certain financial ratios such as a minimum current ratio, and (4) in general, to run the business in accordance with plans outlined in the loan application.

V.   A *negative covenants section* in which the borrower promises that without prior written consent of the lender that the borrower will not do certain things like (1) sell assets, (2) pay dividends above an agreed upon amount, (3) increase individual officer salaries in excess of certain percentages, (4) guarantee obligations of others, or (5) pledge any of its assets to another lender.

VI. An *events of default section* that defines events that constitute default on the part of the borrower that will allow the lender to accelerate the debt and call his note. Such events could include (1) bankruptcy, (2) failure to meet note payments, and (3) violation of covenants in the agreement.

Guarantees

Businessmen routinely are required to personally guarantee payment of loan obligations of the business they own and operate. It is only reasonable to do so if you own the business or are in a position to control its operation. Moreover, guarantees add your personal financial strength to back the loan, and your guarantee may add the necessary financial strength for you to get a loan. Most lenders have their own standard guarantee forms, but guarantees can be tailor-made. Consult your attorney if you have questions on guarantees that you are asked to sign.

Waivers

A *waiver* simply is a foregoing of one's rights to something. Suppose that you rent the building that your business uses for its operation and that you wish to take out a loan for new and existing equipment now in or to be put in the building. The lender will require you to get a *landlord's waiver* that waives his rights under your lease agreement with him whereby he could attach your equipment and leasehold improvements and fixtures if you do not meet your lease payments. Be sure that you understand any waiver that you sign.

Subordination Agreements

A subordination agreement simply means that one lender agrees to subordinate his claim on the assets of a business to the claims of another lender. For instance, if you have made loans to your business, a bank or other lender probably will ask you to subordinate your claim or note to their loans.

Insurance Agreements

An important part of many loan agreements is the provision that requires the borrower to maintain adequate property and casualty insurance. Also, some agreements specify that the borrower will maintain adequate life insurance of key personnel in the firm. With respect to property and casualty insurance, the loan agreement will require that the lender be named as loss payee. That is, if pledged property is lost due to any insured risk, then the lender would be paid by the insurance company. With respect to life insurance, the lender may require the policies on key personnel to be assigned to the lender. If adequate insurance is not in force, then more must be purchased. One of the indirect benefits of borrowing a significant amount of money is that it will force you to reevaluate your entire risk management and insurance program.

CLOSING THE LOAN

Document Preparation

Prior to the loan closing and getting the money you need, the necessary loan documents must be drawn and be in proper order for execution. As mentioned previously, documentation is not a clear-cut standardized proposition. Documentation ranges from the simple unsecured working capital note to complicated term loans with many kinds of collateral. Depending on the complexity of the loan, your attorney will be working with you and the loan officer and his attorney to get the loan documents in proper form for closing.

Delivery of Documents

As individual documents are prepared, they should be mutually agreed upon by all parties so that no confusion or last minute modification is required when the closing takes place.

Document Execution

The process of document execution is commonly known as the *loan closing*. At the closing all interested parties (borrower, lender, and attorneys) meet and sign the loan documents.

Filing for Record

Immediately after the closing, the attorneys will record mortgages and file other notices for public record.

Attorney's Opinion -SIDE

At closing and after filing for record, the lender will require your attorney's opinion that everything that has been done is authorized and legal and that all filing and recordings effect the agreed upon security interests to the lender.

Disbursements - SIDE

After closing and filing, the lender will let you have the money either by giving you a check or crediting your checking account.

SUMMARY

The key point in this chapter is that the loan closing is a detailed, complex process. There is no way that you can be an expert in it. In fact, at the loan closing you probably will be the most inexperienced person in attendance. If you learn the steps described in this chapter and consult with experts such as your attorney and accountant you should have no problem at the closing.

After the loan has been approved and all the terms and conditions have been agreed to by both you and the lender, then the process of closing the loan begins.

Conclusion -

The loan closing is a detailed, complex process. There is no way that one can be an expert in borrowing money without having experienced the process. However, if you follow a few basic steps and consult with experts there should be no problems that can not be solved.

8
What Happens After You Get the Money

After you receive the money from the lender, do not be under the misconception that you can "kiss him goodbye" and just mail checks in when they are due. Remember, when you received the money, you also picked up a new partner in your business. You had better believe that your new partner wants to stay informed about how the business is doing.

In many ways, what you do after you get the money is the most important part of borrowing. It is your chance to prove that you can do everything that you promised that you would do throughout the entire borrowing process. It also is your chance to prove your abilities as a manager. You must demonstrate that you can generate sales shown in your *pro forma* income statement, that you can control costs, that you can collect your receivables, and that you can generate adequate profits.

In essence, you do four things after you get the money: (1) comply with the terms of the documents and loan agreements, (2) perform in your business, (3) monitor your performance, and (4) provide financial information to the lender. You probably had thought of these post-loan functions; however, they are so important to your present and future financial well-being that we decided to emphasize them by featuring them in a separate chapter.

COMPLY WITH THE LOAN AGREEMENT

Checklist of Action Items

At the loan closing, you should receive copies of every document. We suggest if there is a loan agreement that you take it and make a separate list of every item in it that requires action on your part. Checklists will vary according to the terms of various agreements. A sample checklist for the first year is shown on page 109.

Next, set up a file for this loan and place all documents in it with the checklist on top. You will receive notice when property taxes, insurance premiums, and loan payments are due. So it is just a matter of having your bookkeeper remit on time. The same is true for financial statements. Instruct your bookkeeper to send copies of quarterly financial statements to the lender. Those borrowers with a tickler system card file may have cards made for all reporting dates. It also would pay you to review the loan agreement periodically to remind yourself of the negative covenants—those things that you have agreed not to do without the lender's written permission.

Importance of Compliance

It is in your best interest to comply with all terms and conditions of the loan documents and keep the lender informed. If you do not, the lender has a right to call the loan under the terms of the default section of the agreement. Having the lender call the loan would be disastrous for your business because you would not have the cash to pay the loan in full. Even if you sold assets to raise the necessary cash, such action would have an adverse effect on your business operations. Moreover, this bad credit experience would be included in your credit record with the lender and credit reporting agencies. If future credit inquiries are made, the lender's credit department would inform the lenders how you performed. Other prospective lenders are going to reason from this information that you may not comply with conditions of their loans.

Suppose that your suppliers get the word that you reneged with a lender. Such information might jeopardize your ability to buy inventory or materials on credit. With a lessened ability to use trade credit, you might need to borrow additional money that you had not planned on. In short, noncompliance with a loan documents and agreements spells PROBLEMS! Try to imagine what problems might have come out of the woodwork if you had not complied with terms and conditions of previous loans.

The above paragraph is concerned with negatives; however there are a number of positive benefits to be derived from strict and prompt compliance with loan documents and agreements. First, compliance allows you to build a clean record with the lender. The next time that you ask to renew a line of credit or seek long-term financing, you will be ahead of the game. The lender already will know about your ability and willingness to handle credit properly.

Second, if you need a long-term mortgage or some other type of financing from another lender, when he calls the first lender he will be told that you paid on time and complied with the terms and conditions of the loan and any agreement.

Third, suppose that much later, you decide to "go public" by offering shares in your company to outside investors. When investment bankers review your financial situation and find a solid record of compliance with loan terms and conditions, they will be more inclined to underwrite the stock issue.

What we are trying to stress here is that your record of noncompliance or compliance with loan terms and conditions will follow you for a long time. A good credit will pay positive dividends to you and your business. A poor record can be extremely difficult to overcome.

MONITOR YOUR PERFORMANCE

In order to comply with your loan terms and agreements, you must monitor your firm's operational and financial performance. The occasion of a new loan is a good time to review every aspect of your operational and financial control systems. With your new "partner" aboard there is new and added pressure on you to produce efficiently and to make sure cash is on hand to make payments on schedule.

Checklist of Action Items in the Loan Agreement

1. Submit Financial Statements

                                   Date of Compliance

    (a) June 30   _____

    (b) September 30   _____

    (c) December 31   _____

    (d) March 31   _____

2. Pay Property Taxes

    (a) December 31   _____

3. Pay Semiannual Property and Casualty Insurance Premiums

    (a) April 27   _____

    (b) October 27   _____

4. Pay Semiannual Life Insurance Premiums on Key People

    (a) September 10   _____

    (b) March 10   _____

5. Make Loan Payments

	Principal Payment	Interest Payment	Principal Remaining	Date
(a) June 30	_____	_____	_____	____
(b) September 30	_____	_____	_____	____
(c) December 31	_____	_____	_____	____
(d) March 31	_____	_____	_____	____

Operational Performance

Review production and sales records to see if there are any ways that you can be more efficient in the operation of your business. Such a review means that you look for ways to produce or sell more with the same resources and costs, or produce the same amount with less resources and costs. Either way, the ratio of output to input increases and your business will become more efficient and profitable.

In recent times, productivity or output per man-hour in the United States has grown very little and, in some years, it declined. Increasing productivity is the source of any increase in real income. In the long run, you cannot pay people for what they do not produce. As a nation, we cannot consume if we do not produce. Stated differently, "there ain't no such thing as a free lunch." If someone eats, someone had to produce!

There are several reasons for declines in productivity. First, the average experience level in the labor force is down because of the influx of inexperienced workers, namely older women, into the labor force. Second, in recent years there has been change in societal values toward work. People just do not want to work as hard as they once did. There are a lot of people with an "I deserve" type of attitude around. Today, it is estimated that unauthorized absences from work account for 100 million hours of lost production time every week. Third, the time off for holidays, vacations, coffee breaks, maternity leave, office parties, etc., generate a lot of paid time, but no product. Last, the rate of new investment in plant and equipment has slowed considerably. Experts on productivity tell us that the primary reason for the tremendous historical increase in productivity in this country has been that American workers were provided with more and more capital assets to work with. Hence, the declining rate of capital investment has led to declining productivity.

We point out the "productivity problem" so that you can take action to prevent it from undermining production in your plant or store and, hence, your ability to meet your financial obligations. With respect to the problem of inexperienced workers, try to hire people with experience. With respect to your employees' attitude toward work, tell them that the highest pay increases will go to those that produce or sell the most. This is a corollary of that time-honored economic principle, "thems that work gets paid." Finally, with respect to lost time due to holidays, vacations, coffee breaks, etc., there is nothing that one firm can do to alter the number of national holidays. Moreover, the break provided by a vacation helps to restore individual productivity. However, a business can reduce lost time from other diversions such as office parties with clear policies that they not be held on employee time. A profit-seeking business is not a charity! Note that the first three reasons offered for declining productivity can be corrected with no monetary outlay. Good management can right these problems.

Financial Performance

Monitoring a firm's financial performance is just as important as keeping a close tab on production. You might be able to argue that it is more important.

Good financial management and control begin with accurate record keeping. Remember the old "garbage in, garbage out" principle. If your records are no good, then you cannot manage your firm properly.

Profit Planning

Monitoring financial performance is an important step in profit planning. *Profit planning* essentially is a managerial process designed to achieve a firm's profit objectives. An important part of profit planning is the development of a formal *profit plan,* which is a written statement in both financial and nonfinancial terms of a firm's profit objectives. The usual time to draw up a profit plan is just before the end of your fiscal year when you have a good idea about the current year's results and, therefore, can outline next year's profit objectives.

The first step in profit planning is to set your net profit objective for the year, for example, $100,000. Second, estimate annual gross income from sales and other sources and the annual amount for each expense item. Third, subtract expenses from income and compare the after tax profit total with your objective. Fourth, if the profit objective total is higher than the estimated amount, develop alternative strategies to reduce estimated expenses and/or raise estimated income. Fifth, after the new estimates are made, make a final draft and adopt it as your financial game plan for the coming year. Sixth, monitor and measure the results over the year and take action to keep profits on target.

This last step is the key to the profit planning process. Do not salve your conscience by drafting the plan and sticking it in a file. Each month have your bookkeeper complete a profit plan report that shows (1) *planned amounts* for each income and expense item, (2) *actual amount* for each item, and (3) the *variance* or difference between each item. By using individual variances as an indication of areas where improvements might be effected, look for ways to reduce expense overages and increase lagging sources of income.

Monitoring Cash

Making a profit is necessary to stay in business, but it will not guarantee that you will have the cash to pay your loan on time. Think of cash as a stream that runs through your business. You add to the stream by making sales and collecting receivables. You reduce the stream when you buy raw materials or inventory and pay expenses. We recognized the cash management function in Chapter 2 and outlined there how to construct a cash budget. Remember, a cash budget is a plan to help you manage. It does not tell you what to do with cash on a daily basis. To monitor cash daily have your bookkeeper prepare a daily *cash receipts and disbursements* report that shows receipts, expenditures, and the current cash balance. If your current cash balance begins to rise above the target amount for your bank account, call the bank if you have a line of credit there and ask the note teller to debit (decrease) your account and apply the funds to your outstanding loan balance. Or transfer excess funds to an interest-bearing savings account. Of course, if current cash dips below the targeted balance, call on your line of credit at the bank or commercial finance company. At the end of the month, your bookkeeper can prepare a summary of all inflows and outflows of cash. Compare the individual totals with the cash budget. On the basis of this comparison, you may wish to adjust future monthly totals in the original cash budget.

The focus of the previous paragraph was on monitoring cash over the monthly cash cycle. If you have a loan that requires a large quarterly, semiannual, or annual payment, you need to accumulate cash over the period to make this payment. Many loan agreements do not call for prepayment penalties if you pay ahead of time. So if you accumulate a reasonable sum of cash that you know is not needed in the regular short-term operation of the business, you might make a partial payment toward the large installment and thereby reduce interest expense. Alternatively, you may accumulate the money in a business savings account or in a money market mutual fund that pays daily interest and allows you to make withdrawals when the money is needed.

PROVIDE FINANCIAL AND OTHER INFORMATION

Virtually all loan agreements will require that you provide the lender with periodic financial information in the form of annual statements of condition and income statements. It is a good idea to send these in promptly and not wait for a reminder from the lender. If your business is new or not in top-flight financial condition, the lender may require that statements be prepared and submitted on a more frequent basis. This will be more costly to you, but you benefit by keeping the lender informed and happy. If you have your accounts on computer, this will facilitate the task.

Besides financial information, send your lender memos or letters that keep him apprised of other developments in the company. This means both the "bad news" as well as the "good news." For example, if a strike shuts down a major supplier and your production or sales begin to suffer because you cannot get the goods, inform the lender of the problem. If your sales manager is out four weeks because of illness and sales begin to slide, inform your lender. Just use good judgment and common sense in deciding what to tell the lender.

Lenders do not like to be surprised by finding out something

themselves that you should have told them or by your delaying un-
necessarily in telling them some bad news. Lenders interpret this
just like you would if your sales manager failed to tell you for two
weeks that the firm had lost a major account. "Lay your cards on
the table!" Be open and above board with the lender. He knows
that things are not always rosy in his business or yours. KEEP
THE LENDER INFORMED!

SUMMARY

Here are the key points in this chapter:

1. To ensure strict and timely compliance with the terms of
    your loan agreement, set up a checklist of action items.
2. Monitor your operational performance to ensure that pro-
    ductivity and efficiency are maintained.
3. Monitor your financial performance with the use of a viable
    profit plan, a daily cash receipt and disbursements summary
    sheet, and a cash budget.
4. Keep the lender informed with timely and accurate state-
    ments of condition and income statements and other rele-
    vant facts (good and bad) about your business.

9

Financial Management During Tough Times

Up to this point the thrust of the book has been on how to help you find the money you need to run your business over the cash cycle or to expand over a longer period. Except for a few caveats dropped here and there, the general implications between the lines was that all you had to do was to put up some of your capital, borrow some from a lender, hang out your shingle, and live happily ever after. We wish that it were this easy.

In recent years, it has become increasingly difficult for experienced as well as inexperienced business managers to succeed in business. In view of this fact we would be remiss if we did not try to offer some words of wisdom to help you survive financially during tough times. If you have survived, then we are sure that you could offer some sage advice. The primary purposes of this chapter are: (1) discuss the reasons for tough times, (2) explain the financial difficulties that you may encounter, and (3) provide some proven action steps to take for sound financial management.

REASONS FOR TOUGH TIMES

Inflation
Inflation is a sustained increase in the general level of prices. In the recent past the United States has experienced several years of

double-digit inflation and an average annual inflation rate of more than double the long-run trend in effect since the first part of this century.

Inflation can be traced primarily to a too-rapid expansion of the money supply. In a nutshell, inflation is caused by "too much money chasing too few goods and services." At times, the Federal Reserve (Fed), the part of our government in charge of managing the money supply, has allowed it to grow too rapidly in order to encourage economic expansion and reduce unemployment. Most of the time, the Fed has achieved its goals of a growing Gross National Product (GNP) and low unemployment, but it has been at a price—inflation.

Inflation affects a business on both the income and expense sides of the income statement. During inflationary periods, a business usually is able to raise it prices. To what extent it can raise its prices depends on the degree of competition that it faces and the demand for the firm's products or services. A firm operating in a market with many competitors may have difficulty pushing up prices. Also, from the demand side of the market, if prices are raised the quantity of goods or services that the public wants may decrease so sharply that the firm decides that it is better off by not raising prices.

On the other hand, the extent to which a firm's expenses rise depends on the degree of competition for the product or services from other firms and the ability of firms that supply the product or service to provide it. For example, the cost of ballpoint pens barely increased during the recent inflation. This is because the demand for ballpoint pens has increased very little, because improvements in technology have allowed pen manufacturers to increase production with very little costs, and because the supply of felt-tipped pens, which compete with ballpoint pens, has increased very sharply. On the other hand, the cost of gasoline, which is an important cost at every firm, has skyrocketed well above the average rate of inflation. As we all know, the supply of this scarce resource has been limited by producers while at the same time the demand for it from all sectors of the economy has remained strong.

Thus, how well an individual business survives inflation depends on the extent to which it can raise prices and the extent to which it can control costs. Generally, during inflation, a firm has very limited control over either side of the income statement. Sure you can increase your efforts to sell more, but competition will limit your success. Also you can try to be more efficient and reduce your purchases of products and services that you utilize in the business. However, you can cut back only so much.

Unfortunately the forecast for inflation is bad. Experts fear that inflation will average eight to nine percent in the 1980s. This means that prices will double between 1980 and 1988-1989. The obvious question is: What can be done about it? Answer: The American public has to decide that inflation must cease. This message must be heard in Washington by the Fed, Congress, and the President. The Fed has the tools to halt inflation, but Congress and the President must not interfere with the Fed's ability to deal with the problem by imposing laws and requirements that hinder it. Remember, one house of Congress turns over every two years and the other house turns over every six years. Unfortunately, the primary objective of our elected representatives appears to be to win reelection. Sometimes this causes them to put pressure on the Fed to gun the money supply too rapidly. When this happens, the people lose. Until the problem of inflation is licked, business is going to have some tough times.

High Interest Rates

Another sign of these tough times is the highest interest rates in the history of the country. The prime rate hit 21.5 percent in 1980 with many nonprime borrowers financing inventory and receivables at up to 25 percent. Construction and development loans are carrying interest rates of like amounts. You do not have to be a mental giant to figure out that interest rates like these cut the heart out of profit margins.

Why are interest rates so high? Inflation is the primary cause. When inflationary expectations rise, interest rates increase because of the actions of both demanders and suppliers of funds. The anticipation of inflation will cause many businesses to seek funds in the money and capital markets in order to purchase inventory plant, equipment, and other real assets before they rise in price. This surge in demand for funds pushes up interest rates.

Regarding supply, if lenders also anticipate inflation they will demand higher interest rates in order to offset the expected inflation. The amount that interest rates rise above a before inflation "real rate of interest" is called the *inflation premium*. If interest rates rise to 15 percent, generally demanders and suppliers of funds must be expecting an inflation rate in the vicinity of 12-13 percent.

Thus, inflation is the real culprit behind high interest rates. If we could bring inflation under control, interest rates would decline and tend to stabilize.

Recession

The prototype of a tough time was the Great Depression when the GNP fell by 50 percent and 25 percent of the labor force was unemployed. Fortunately, since World War II we have not had another Great Depression—but we have had periods of recession. Economists define *recession* as two consecutive quarters of declining GNP. During such times, unemployment increases and the economic welfare of our people declines.

The economy suffered its worst postwar recession between November 1973 and March 1975. Unemployment reached nine percent and for several months in 1974 and 1975, industrial production fell at an annual rate of 22 percent. The 1973-1975 recession was so severe that it made all of us realize that tough times could hit us even though most of us lived in nice houses, were well-fed, and drove air-conditioned automobiles.

Periodic recessions with the prospect of declining sales, profits, and loan defaults are a real fear for every business. President Johnson once said that "we had legislated away the business cycle." But, unfortunately, that is not true. Our economy seems destined to experience periodic recessions and slowdowns. Why is this? The primary reason is the stop-start rate of growth in the money supply. Since 1867, every major and minor economic decline has been preceded by a slowdown in the rate of growth in the money supply. Until the Fed is able to increase the money supply smoothly and in line with growth in the real economy, business will continue to experience disruptive tough times from recessions.

Declining Productivity

We already have mentioned the problem of declining productivity and it is listed here only to remind you that it must share part of the responsibility for the tough times experienced recently by businesses. When many of your employees think that they deserve pay increases without commensurate productivity increases, then times are tough.

Energy Crunch

The steep rise in the cost of gasoline, natural gas, and utility bills has put great pressure on business profit margins. There is no way that American businesses can raise their prices to cover fully the increases in energy costs. Therefore, profit margins have shrunk. No one knows how many marginal businesses have been forced into bankruptcy because of rising energy costs.

At this time prospects of resolving the energy crunch seem dim. In the past, American technology always solved our problems. Perhaps it can now. But prior to that time, there is a good chance that energy shortages could create some very tough times for business. For example, suppose for some reason that 40 percent of our oil sources were shut off. It would be disastrous for every business. Let's hope that this does not happen.

International Tension

Since World War II, we have experienced hot and cold wars. The Korean War and the Vietnam War caused serious disruptions in our economy. However, the Berlin crisis, the Suez crises, the Lebanon crisis, the Cuban Missile crisis, the Israeli-Egyptian conflicts, the Iranian crisis, and the Soviet invasion of Afghanistan all impacted in one way or another on businesses. In the future, it seems certain that a pattern of crises, flareups, and open wars will continue. The world population is heading toward six billion by the year 2000 and at the same time the supply of known resources is shrinking; this can only create tension as people fight to survive. We do not want to get carried away with the gloom and doom theme, but the environment in which you do business will be shaped and conditioned by the underlying reality of an expanding population and scarce resources.

DIFFICULTIES YOU CAN INCUR IN TOUGH TIMES

In the discussion above, we gave several examples of ways in which tough times impact on business. In this section let's consider specifically the difficulties that the above problems cause for business.

1. *Increased risk.* Financial risk may be defined either as the possibility of loss of profits or the negative variability in profits. Either way you define it, tough times increase risk for businesses. Both income and expenses become less certain and, hence, increase the possibility of loss and increase the variability in profits from a business. Combine this condition with the highly publicized fact that even in normal times 80 percent of all new businesses fail within five years and you can easily see that the chance of business survival in tough times is even less.

2. *High cost of money.* As explained earlier, anticipated inflation has pushed interest rates to record levels. This means that the high cost of funds for short-and long-term purposes is squeezing profit margins. This fact places a burden on you to manage your interest-bearing liabilities (loans) more closely, especially if your interest rate floats.

3. *Lenders become more selective.* Lenders are well aware of tough times because they have to deal with their own liquidity and profit squeeze. Moreover, from their experience in dealing with other borrowers who are in trouble, they have a pretty good feel for what you and other business managers are having to do to survive. During tough times, every lender's loan losses rise. This fact makes lenders more selective in choosing their borrowers. You can bet your last dollar that marginal and risky businesses will be weeded out and not receive the money they seek.

4. *Sales level off.* During tough times, many firms find that sales level off as consumers become more cautious and businesses react by not expanding their investment in plant and equipment. You should try to expand sales through increased efforts, but beware of being so zealous that you cut prices to levels that do not cover costs. Do not give your goods and services away!

5. *Inventories accumulate.* A by-product of a sales slowdown is the accumulation of inventory. Moreover, this inventory pile-up usually coincides with periods of high interest rates which means the cost of carrying inventory is high.

6. *Receivables become difficult to collect.* During tough times, you find out who can pay and who cannot. Customers squeezed for cash will delay and make all kinds of excuses why they cannot pay on time.

7. *Trade creditors want faster payment.* At the same time you find that your receivables are more difficult to collect, your trade creditors will begin to demand faster payment from you. They may demand payment when goods are delivered or, in extreme cases, prior to shipment. When the latter occurs, you know times are tough.

8. *Profits are squeezed.* The usual result of everything bad described so far in this chapter is that profits are squeezed and, hence, your ability to pay debt is reduced.

ACTIONS TO TAKE FOR FINANCIAL SURVIVAL DURING TOUGH TIMES

Knute Rockne's famous line to his Notre Dame team at half-time was, "when the going get tough, the tough get going." Nothing could be more true for the business world when inflation, high interest, and an energy crunch hits you high and low. When times are tough, you have to tighten your belt, think positively, and take action. In this section, we want to list a number of action steps that you can take to deal with the problems described earlier.

1. *Monitor cash closely.* Action step number one during tough times has to be to monitor cash closely. In times like these, everyone is short of cash. Your loans have to be paid in cash. Your lenders do not want to be paid with inventory receivables, or used equipment. They want dollars! Remember cash is a stream

that flows through your business. Keep a close tab on cash flow with your daily cash receipts and disbursements report.

2. *Do not pay until you have to, but take all trade discounts.* The advice here is to hold your cash and pay invoices and statements on the last day. We are not advising you do anything wrong; just do precisely what the terms of credit call for. However, if the terms of credit call for trade discounts, by all means take them. It costs you nearly 37 percent not to take a 2/10 net 30 discount.

3. *Tighten credit policy and practices.* During tough times, do not sell to high-risk credit customers in order to boost sales. A fundamental business principle is that "a sale is not complete until you collect the money." If you try to boost sales and profits by loosening credit standards, you are only deceiving yourself; more than likely the losses sustained from such a policy will decrease profit. Therefore, make sure that new customers complete a credit application and that you review it as thoroughly as your lenders reviewed yours.

4. *Beef up collection efforts.* In the collection of receivables, there is not much room for nice guys. Be tough and stay after past due accounts. Think of a receivable as your money that you are allowing someone else to hold, probably without interest. Once you realize this, then undoubtedly you will step up your collection efforts. Also consider adding service charges to past due accounts.

5. *Control inventory and purchase levels.* During tough times, pare inventory to the bone. With high interest rates, the cost of carrying inventory is high. Monitor purchases closely. When salesmen call on you, resist the temptation to stock up on items with the low probability of sale. Avoid "stock out" situations by matching purchases and sales very closely. Use this opportunity to sell off dead inventory. Every business has its "dogs and clunkers" sitting around. Chartreuse dresses, dented appliances, and scratched furniture are good examples of items that sit around in a store until the manager wakes up, cuts the price, and moves them out.

6. *Sell nonessential assets.* You can raise cash during tough

times by selling off nonessential assets such as excess equipment. Other businesses might have a use for it because they cannot afford to buy new models. If your firm owns real estate that you acquired for possible future expansion, you might consider selling it to raise cash. In a word, go over your balance sheet and get rid of nonessential nonproductive assets.

7. *Cut overhead.* Reevaluate every item of fixed or indirect costs. Determine if any expense item can be cut. For example, use tough times as the motivation to install a timer on your hot water heater or a more accurate thermostat for the heating system. More than likely you can reduce your photocopying expense. If you can get by with one less secretary, use a resignation as an opportunity not to fill the position. Consolidate the secretarial work. There are hundreds of little things that you can do to minimize waste and cut overhead. Just look around.

8. *Monitor your profit plan closely.* Your profit plan is the guide for managing the bottom line profits. Be persistent and find out why a variance exists in any income or expense item.

9. *Consider leasing instead of buying.* During tough times, it may be more prudent to lease than buy some equipment, even though the cost may be higher. If you really have your back to the wall, this allows you to keep your bank or finance company lines available for essential short-term working capital needs.

10. *Supervise productivity closely.* Inform your employees that times are tough and that you will not tolerate slackers and unauthorized absences. Ask them to study their own job and find ways to be more productive and efficient.

DEALING WITH LENDERS IN TOUGH TIMES

Keep Lenders Informed

In Chapter 8 we emphasized that you should keep your lenders informed. This is even more important in tough times than in good times. Remember lenders do not like to be surprised, and they are much more apt to work with you if they feel that you have not tried to hide anything or pull the wool over their eyes.

Modification and Extension
Do not be afraid to ask for a modification or extension of the terms of outstanding loans. Lenders have ways in which to modify a loan agreement. If you are keeping your lender informed of your financial condition, he probably will suggest ways to help you before you request assistance.

Use Your Lender as A Consultant
An experienced lender has access to a lot of information that you do not have. In tough times, he deals every day with businesses that cannot meet their payments on time. Moreover, he hears things from his contacts with other business managers that could help you survive. For example, your lender might know a firm that needs to liquidate an inventory of items that you could sell. You might be able to buy quality goods at 35 cents on the dollar, sell them for a large profit, and keep your business running smoothly while others are struggling. Every lender has his stories about how he helped Firm A and Firm B by matching their individual needs.

SUMMARY
Here are the key points in this chapter:

1. Inflation, high interest rates, recession, declining productivity, the energy crunch, and international tension, individually and collectively, create tough times for business.

2. As a business manager, you may incur the following difficulties:

   (a) Increased risk
   (b) Higher cost of money
   (c) More selective lenders
   (d) Leveling of sales
   (e) Accumulation of inventory
   (f) Difficulties in collecting receivables
   (g) Request for faster payment from trade creditors
   (h) A profit squeeze

3. The following action steps will help you survive:

   (a) Monitor cash closely
   (b) Do not pay until you have to, but take all trade discounts
   (c) Tighten credit policy and practice
   (d) Beef up collection efforts
   (e) Control inventory and purchase levels
   (f) Sell nonessential assets
   (g) Cut overhead
   (h) Consider leasing instead of buying
   (i) Supervise productivity closely

Glossary*

accounts receivable loan. A short-term loan to finance a short-term increase in accounts receivable. (2, 4)

acid test or quick ratio. $= \dfrac{\text{current assets - inventories}}{\text{current liabilities}}$. (5)

affirmative covenants. Promises by the borrower to perform certain actions either automatically or at the request of the lender. An example of an affirmative covenant is the maintenance of capital. (4)

agreement. Any document used in the loan process. (7)

assets. Things owned and/or claims on value by an individual or business.

attorney's opinion. A written statement by an attorney that everything done in connection with the loan transaction is authorized and legal and that all filing and recordings perfect the agreed-upon security interests to the lender. (7)

average collection period ratio. $= \dfrac{\text{receivables x 360}}{\text{annual credit sales}}$. (5)

balance sheet. A listing of assets, liabilities, and net worth of a person, business, or organization as of a specific date. The balance sheet equation is: assets = liabilities + net worth. (2)

---

*Numbers in parentheses after each item indicate the chapter in which the concept is discussed.

balloon payment. The last and usually substantially larger payment on a loan whose repayment provisions called for smaller and perhaps unequal payments earlier.

business history. An overview of a business from inception to present date. (5)

business risk. The risk of a business loss or failure. (6)

capital budget. A ranking of a business' proposed investment projects in descending order of their worth to the firm. (3)

capital budgeting. The process of planning those expenditures that will benefit a business beyond one year. (3)

cash budgeting. The process of estimating inflows and outflows of cash for a given period or periods of time in order to estimate or forecast cash inflows or needs. (2)

cash cycle. A process whereby cash is used to purchase raw materials which are manufactured into inventory which, when sold, creates accounts receivable which, when collected, becomes cash again. (2)

certificates of deposit (CD's). Interest-bearing time deposits with a fixed maturity, evidenced by a written contract and usually issued in denominations of $100,000 or more, although small denominations are common. (2)

check. An order to a funds holder to pay funds to the payee designated on the check.

closing (loan). The process of document execution prior to the lender paying the loan proceeds to the borrower. (7)

collateral. Assets pledged to secure a loan. (5)

commercial finance company. A business that lends primarily to businesses to finance their accounts receivable, inventory, and sometimes buildings and equipment. (4)

commercial loan. A loan to a business.

commercial paper. Short-term promissory notes sold in the money market by prime-rated businesses. (4)

commitment fee. A charge for the unused portion of a loan. (4)

compensating balance. A sum of money deposited with a creditor that serves as partial compensation to the lender for the loan. (2)

compliance. The borrower's carrying out of the terms and stipulations in the loan agreement. (8)

conditional sales contracts. Contracts for the sale of an asset by a seller where title is retained by the seller until all payments are made. (7)

cosigner. A maker of a note who has the obligation to pay if any other maker fails to pay. (7)

credit. The obligation to pay money in the future.

credit analysis. The process by which a lender evaluates a loan application. (6)

creditor. An individual or business or other organization that allows goods, services, or money to be used in anticipation of future payment for their use.

credit risk. The chance of nonpayment of an obligation to pay money at its due date; the possibility of loss to a lender because of failure of a borrower to pay. (6)

current assets. Assets such as inventory and accounts receivable that normally are converted into cash within a year.

current liabilities. Obligations to pay cash within one year.

current ratio. $= \dfrac{\text{current assets}}{\text{current liabilities}}$. (5)

debtor. An individual, business, or other organization that uses goods, services, or money under a promise of future payments for their use.

debt-to-assets ratio. $= \dfrac{\text{total liabilities}}{\text{total assets}}$. (6)

debt-to-equity ratio. $= \dfrac{\text{total liabilities}}{\text{owner's equity}}$. (6)

depreciation. An annual reduction in the book value of a fixed asset that reflects its declining usefulness in the production of income. On the income statement, depreciation is a noncash expense charge against income.

disbursement (loan). The actual payment by the lender of the loan proceeds to the borrower. (7)

factoring. The sale of accounts receivable to a factoring company. (4)

gross profit margin. $= \dfrac{\text{net sales - cost of goods sold}}{\text{net sales}}$. (5)

guarantor (limited). A guarantor of a note who is obligated to pay only a specific amount if any other maker fails to pay. (7)

guarantor (unlimited). A guarantor of a note who must make all missed payments if any other maker fails to pay. (7)

hypothecation (of collateral). A written agreement that permits a borrower to use collateral owned by a third party to secure the borrower's loan.

income statement. A list of income and expenses incurred by a person or a business over a period of time, such as a year. (2)

individual transaction loans. Loans for a specific purpose for a specific period of time, usually of less than one year. (4)

inflation. A sustained increase in the general level of prices. (9)

inflation premium (in interest rates). The extent to which stated or nominal interest rates exceed the "real rate of interest." For example, if the real rate of interest is 3 percent and the stated interest rate on a loan is 12 percent, the inflation premium is 9 percent. (9)

insurance agreement. An agreement whereby a borrower agrees to maintain adequate property and casualty insurance. Sometimes insurance agreements specify that the borrower must maintain adequate life insurance on key personnel in the business. (7)

interest. A charge for the use of money. (4)

interest coverage ratio. $= \dfrac{\text{income before interest and income taxes}}{\text{interest charges}}$. (5)

inventory loan. A short-term loan used to finance a short-term increase in inventory. (2, 4)

inventory turnover ratio. $= \dfrac{\text{cost of goods sold}}{\text{average inventory}}$. (5)

landlord waiver. An agreement whereby a landlord foregoes his rights under a lease agreement to attach equipment and lease-hold improvements and fixtures. (7)

lease-purchase contract. An agreement whereby the leasee agrees to buy the leased asset at the end of the lease in accordance with an agreed or stipulated price. (7)

leasing. Use of an asset for a fee. (4)

leverage (financial). The extent to which a business has used borrowed funds to finance assets. (6)

liabilities. Obligations of individuals or businesses to pay for things owned or services rendered.

liquidity (of a firm). The ability of a business to pay its maturing liabilities with cash.

line of credit. An informal arrangement whereby a lender agrees to lend to a business up to some amount, such as $100,000 during a period such as year. This lending arrangement is usually governed by stipulated terms and conditions. (2, 4)

long-term credit. A loan or other extension of credit that is to be paid in a period of longer than one year. (3)

money. Anything commonly used and generally accepted in exchange for goods and services and for the payment of debts. (2)

money market mutual fund shares. Participation by investment of money in a fund that is managed by a broker. The fund consists of CDs and other short-term securities that pay daily interest, and it may permit shareholders to redeem shares by writing a draft on the account. (2)

near money. Financial claims such as Treasury bills that can be converted quite easily into demand deposits, Federal Reserve notes, and coins. (2)

negative covenants. Promises by the borrower not to perform certain actions without the lender's consent. An example of a negative covenant is the agreement not to encumber further the assets of the business. (4)

negotiable order of withdrawl (NOW). A check-like instrument that directs a transfer of funds from a savings account to the payee of the order. (2)

net present value (NPV) method (of capital budgeting). A technique of ranking investment projects according to the amount of discounted net cash flow generated from the project. (3)

net profit margin. $= \dfrac{\text{net profit}}{\text{sales}}$. (5)

note. A written promise to pay. (7)

participation loan. A loan made by more than one lender. (4)

payback method (of capital budgeting). A technique of ranking investment projects according to how quickly their original cost is recovered from cash flow (net income plus depreciation). (3)

permanent increase in working capital. A higher permanent *level* of working capital associated with a higher permanent *level* of sales.

personal finance company. A business that lends primarily to individuals for consumer purposes. (4)

personal financial statement. A listing of assets, liabilities, and net worth of an individual on a specific date.

precautionary cash balances. Funds held to meet contingencies such as unexpected declines in income or increases in payments. (2)

prime rate. The interest rate generally charged to the most creditworthy borrowers of commercial banks. (4)

profit plan. A written statement in both financial and non-financial terms of a firm's profit objectives. (8)

profit planning. A managerial process designed to achieve a firm's profit objectives. (8)

pro forma statements of condition and income statements. Projected statements of condition and income statements for future periods (usually one to five years). (5)

rate of return on assets. $= \dfrac{\text{net profit}}{\text{total assets - intangible assets}}$. (5)

rate of return on owners' equity. $= \dfrac{\text{net profit}}{\text{owners' equity}}$. (5)

recession. Two consecutive quarters of declining GNP. (9)

revolving credit agreement. A binding legal agreement between borrower and lender. The lender agrees to lend on a continuous basis for a specified period of time provided all covenants of the agreement are met by the borrower. (4)

share draft. A check-like instrument that enables a person to transfer funds from his or her interest-bearing account at a credit union. (2)

short-term credit. A loan or other extension of credit that is to be paid in one year or less. (2)

speculative cash balances. Funds held because at the present the owner does not wish to invest in plant and equipment or some other asset. (2)

subordination agreement. An agreement whereby one lender agrees to subordinate his claim on the assets of a business to the claims of another lender. (7)

term loan. A loan with an initial maturity of one year or more. Term loans are used to finance long-term assets such as plant and equipment and permanent increases in working capital. (4)

terms of sale. Agreed upon terms of remittance in trade credit. (4)

$$\text{\textbf{total debt coverage ratio.}} = \frac{\text{income before interest and income taxes}}{\text{interest} + \text{principal charges} \; (1/1 - \text{combined federal and state tax rates})}. \text{(5)}$$

trade credit. Short-term credit extended by vendors to buyers. (4)

unsecured loans. Loans for which collateral is not pledged. (4)

usury laws. Laws that specify the maximum interest rate that can be charged on various types of loans.

waiver. A foregoing of one's rights to something. (7)

working capital. Equity in current assets. The excess of current assets minus current liabilities.

working capital loans. Short-term loans to finance short-term assets such as inventory and accounts receivable. (5)

Appendix
Interest Computation

WHAT IS INTEREST?

Simply stated, interest is the price paid over time for the use of a lender's money. Some people prefer to say that interest is the time value of money. Every day, individuals, businesses, and governments buy goods and services whose prices are set by the interaction of supply and demand in various markets. The cost of renting money is set in a similar manner, except that the manner in which interest is computed often is very confusing. This primary purpose of this Appendix is to show you how interest charges are calculated. This should enable you to deal more effectively with lenders when the subject of interest comes up in the borrowing process.

Before we look at the various ways of calculating interest, the term usury should be explained. *Usury* is the lending of money at interest rates above the maximum legal rates. Various state and Federal statutes set usury limits. As a borrower you should be acquainted with these statutes. However, most lending institutions are regulated closely and dare not intentionally charge illegal rates.

BASIC INTEREST CALCULATIONS

Simple Interest

Simple interest is the amount of interest charged on a sum of borrowed money for the length of time the money is borrowed.

Example:

Loan—$1000
Time—90 days
Interest—10 percent

Calculations:

$$\text{Interest:} = \frac{\$1,000 \times .10}{4}$$

Interest = $25

At the outset the borrower receives $1,000 and promises to repay this principal plus interest at the end of 90 days. Hence, at the end of 90 days he owes $1,025.

This calculation may seem confusing to some, but remember an interest rate is a *per year* charge. Interest for one year at 10 percent on $1,000 is $100. In this example, the money is to be borrowed for only one-fourth of a year, so the interest charged is divided by 4 to determine the charge to borrow $1,000 for 90 days.

Let's reflect a moment on this example. First, interest was computed for a year and divided by 4 to determine the charge for 90 days. Second, this calculation assumes that one year equals 360 days. Therefore, let's recalculate the interest on $1,000 at 10 percent for 90 days using a 365-day year.

$$\$1000 \times .10 = \$100 \text{ interest per year}$$
$$\$100 \div 365 = \$.274 \text{ (27.4 cents per day)}$$
$$\$.274 \times 90 = \$24.66 \text{ for 90 days}$$

This is 34 cents less per thousand dollars for 90 days than the $25 charges using a 360 day computation. The annual charge is the same (\$.274 x 365 = \$100), but one-fourth of 365 days equals 91.25 days. Interest is not charged for "quarter days," and it is computed usually on the most easily calculated basis. The difference in interest charged is not much, but it does demonstrate that for \$25 you should be able to borrow \$1,000 for 91.25 days rather than 90 days. As the sum borrowed increases, the dollar difference increases. On \$10,000 the difference is \$3.40, and on \$1,000,000 it is \$340. This example should convince you to ask on what basis your interest is calculated and to be aware that a 360 day versus a 365 day calculaton will cost you a slightly higher amount of interest.

Monthly Payment Loans

Simple interest loans may require payment of interest on a monthly, quarterly, semiannual, or annual basis depending on your cash flow and your agreement with the lender. Payment of interest may be handled two ways: (1) a constant principal payment *plus* interest or (2) a constant total payment *including* interest. Below are examples illustrating these payment methods.

Method 1: Constant Principal Payment Plus Interest

MONTH	LOAN BALANCE	PRINCIPAL PAYMENT	PLUS INTEREST[a]	TOTAL PAYMENT
1	\$1200	\$100	\$10.00	\$110.00
2	1100	100	9.17	109.17
3	1000	100	8.33	108.33
4	900	100	7.50	107.50
5	800	100	6.67	106.67
6	700	100	5.83	105.83
7	600	100	5.00	105.00
8	500	100	4.17	104.17
9	400	100	3.33	103.33
10	300	100	2.50	102.50
11	200	100	1.67	101.67
12	100	100	.83	100.83
	0	\$1200	\$65.00	\$1265.00

a Under this method, interest is calculated on the principal amount outstanding at the end of each month.

Method 2: Constant Total Payment Including Interest

MONTH	LOAN BALANCE	PRINCIPAL PAYMENT	PLUS INTEREST [a]	TOTAL PAYMENT
1	$1,200.00	$95.50	$10.00	$105.50
2	1,104.50	96.30	9.20	105.50
3	1,008.20	97.10	8.40	105.50
4	911.11	97.91	7.59	105.50
5	813.20	98.72	6.78	105.50
6	714.47	99.55	5.95	105.50
7	614.93	100.38	5.12	105.50
8	514.55	101.21	4.29	105.50
9	413.34	102.06	3.44	105.50
10	311.28	102.91	2.59	105.50
11	208.38	103.76	1.74	105.50
12	104.62	104.62	.87	105.50
		$1200.00	$65.97	$1266.00

[a]Total does not add to $66 due to rounding.

The total amount paid under Method 2 is $1,266.00 which is slightly higher than under the first method.

The lesson from the above examples should be clear. A constant payment that includes principal and interest will produce a monthly payment that is less in the earlier months (e.g., $110.00 vs. $105.50 in the first month) but higher in the later months (e.g., $100.88 vs. $105.50 in the last month). Higher payments in the latter months on larger loan amounts could have an impact on cash management.

Discounted Interest

Most lenders that lend for short periods of time (less than one year) prefer to discount time notes because discounting increases the effective yield. Discounting is a common and accepted practice, but you should know the difference between simple interest and discounted interest charges.

Suppose that you borrow $1,000 at 10 percent for 1 year. If interest is paid on a simple interest basis, then the borrower gets the full use of the money for 1 year, and he pays $100 in interest. The effective cost to you is 10 percent.

$$\frac{\$100}{\$1000} = .10$$

On the other hand, if the lender discounts the note at the time the note is signed, then interest is paid at that time (in advance), and the borrower receives the use of only $900 over the term of the loan. However, he is obligated to repay the face amount of the note or $1,000, which includes $100 interest. In the case of discounted interest, the effective cost of the money increases from 10 percent to 11.11 percent.

$$\frac{\$100}{\$900} = .1111$$

In a nutshell, you pay interest in *advance* on a discounted loan and *at maturity* on a simple interest loan.

Add-on interest

"Add-on interest" loans are those in which interest is added to the principal at the time the loan is made. Then the resulting sum is divided by the number of months in the term of the loan to determine the monthly payment.

Example:
Loan—$1,200
Time—12 months
Interest—10 percent

Calculations:
Interest at 10 percent for 1 year on $1200 = $120
$1200 plus interest of $120 = $1320
$1320 loan ÷ 12 months = $110 per month

The effective annual interest rate on this loan is 17.97 percent.[1] What happened here? With the add-on interest method, the borrower obtains $1,200, but he signs a note for $1,320 since interest is added on for one full year at the stated interest rate. However, he makes payments monthly, and he does not get the benefit of using the amount he borrowed for the full year. Hence, his rate or cost of borrowing increases.

Lenders using the add-on interest technique should disclose the fact that add-on interest is being used. If the lender does not disclose the method used for interest calculations, you should ask. Add-on interest is most frequently used in financing automobiles, rolling stock, and other equipment.

FIXED AND FLOATING INTEREST RATES

Fixed Rates

A fixed rate loan simply means that the interest rate is set at the time you sign the note, and it will not change. For example, if you borrow $1,000 at 10 percent for one year, 10 percent will be the interest rate over the entire term of the loan.

Floating Rates

With a floating rate loan you agree to pay an interest rate that is not fixed, but will change when interest rates change. Floating rate loans are usually pegged or indexed to the prime rate and change as the prime rate changes.

Suppose you borrow when the prime rate is 10 percent and agree on a rate that will float always at 1 percent over prime as the prime changes up and down. This means that if prime goes to 15 percent, you pay 16 percent, and if prime goes to 5 percent you will pay 6 percent.

Another floating rate concept involves setting the interest rate as a percentage of the prime rate. Let's consider a loan rate that has been set at 110 percent of the prime rate. At the outset, if the

[1]Board of Governors of the Federal Reserve System, *Annual Percentage Rate Tables,* (Washington, D.C.: Board of Governors of the Federal Reserve System). This publication is available at any reputable lender.

prime rate is 10 percent, then the rate will be 11 percent. But, if prime goes to 15 percent you will pay 16.5 percent, not 16 percent. Conversely, if prime drops to 5 percent you will pay only 5.5 percent, not 6 percent.

Many lenders, especially banks, like to use floating rates because their cost of lendable funds fluctuate. Since their cost fluctuate, they want this income to fluctuate so that they can continue to make profits in all money market conditions.

Floating rate loans have obvious implications for borrowers. Since money costs are an extremely important part of financial planning and if rates are headed up and your loan cost fluctuates, you must be prepared to pass higher costs on to your customers.

Fees

A fee can be another cost of borrowing. Fees are usually charged on relatively large loans if formal commitment letters are issued. They will vary from lender to lender and with market conditions. However, fees generally will range from ½ of 1 percent to 1½ of 2 percent of the amount of your loan commitment. Sometimes fees may be used to skirt usury ceilings. Most often, however, fees are simply "reservation charges" for the commitment to lend. If you decide not to go through with the loan you typically will forfeit your fee.

CONCLUSION

This appendix is by no means designed to be a comprehensive technical discussion on interest charges and borrowing costs. Its thrust is to introduce concepts that frequently will be encountered and help you recognize what to expect. In most instances borrowing costs are negotiable to a certain extent, and you certainly can shop among various lenders. Rely on your accountant or other financial counselor for detailed discussions on borrowing costs as each loan transaction arises.

Index

HOW TO BORROW MONEY

By **Oliver G. Wood, Jr.** and
William C. Barksdale, Jr.

Loan requests often fail only because the borrower does not understand the borrowing process. That is why two banking experts with years of experience in analysing and approving loan requests have put together this handbook. They know money is power in business and that it is essential to financial survival. *How to Borrow Money* will help *you* meet your personal or business borrowing needs by giving you techniques that have been proven to work.

This is the only concise easy-to-follow book on the market that fully explains the borrowing process. And it's written in uncomplicated, nontechnical language that will be readily understood even by borrowers without backgrounds in finance.

You'll discover how to apply for the money you need and how to get a lender to respond quickly to your monetary needs. You'll be fully prepared to handle the loan interview and application. The authors tell you what the lender will do with your application, then give you a behind-the-scenes look at the lender's credit and loan analysis process. You'll know what to expect when closing the loan and getting the money — an often confusing part of the loan transaction. Everything that happens after you get the money is also described, including the borrower's responsibilities to the lender once the loan is closed.

Proven action-steps that will help you survive inflation, recession, and high interest rates are given along with tips on how to manage a business and your cash in tough times. Real-life guidelines cover how to determine and meet your short-term and long-term cash needs.